Getting Employees To Fall In Love With Your Company

Getting Employees To Fall In Love With Your Company

JIM HARRIS, Ph.D.

amacom
American Management Association

New York • Atlanta • Boston • Chicago • Kansas City • San Francisco • Washington, D.C.
Brussels • Mexico City • Tokyo • Toronto

This publication is designed to provide accurate and authoritative
information in regard to the subject matter covered. It is sold with the
understanding that the publisher is not engaged in rendering legal,
accounting, or other professional service. If legal advice or other expert
assistance is required, the services of a competent professional person
should be sought.

Library of Congress Cataloging-in-Publication Data

Harris, Jim, 1953–
    Getting employees to fall in love with your company / Jim Harris.
       p. cm.
    Includes bibliographical references and index.
    ISBN 0-8144-7905-7
    1. Personnel management.   2. Employee motivation. I. Title.
HF5549.H33825   1996
658.3'14—dc20   95-52493
                                               CIP

Printing number

20 19 18 17 16 15 14 13 12 11

To my wife,
Brenda,
for her endless encouragement, patience, and support.

To my mother,
Mary,
for filling her children with love, wisdom, and tolerance.

To my sister,
Bambi,
and my brother,
Tom,
who continue to love me in spite of my many faults.

In memory of my father,
Dave,
for his devotion to family, his passion for life,
and his spirit of independence.

Contents

Acknowledgments

Winston Churchill once said, "Writing a book is an adventure; to begin with it is a toy and an amusement, then it becomes a master, and then it becomes a tyrant; and . . . just as you are about to be reconciled to your servitude—you kill the monster and fling him . . . to the public." As I fling this book to the public, I must acknowledge many of those who have encouraged and facilitated this adventure.

My deepest thanks to Adrienne Hickey at AMACOM. From the beginning, you supported me, guided me, challenged me, and believed in me. Your advice in the final drafts of this manuscript to "lighten up and tighten up" has become my unofficial professional motto.

I have been blessed with countless mentors. To my good friend Dr. Ed Nolan, I offer my ceaseless thanks for allowing me to join your staff and for your continuing tutelage and support. Thank you, Gordie Allen, for guiding me through the jungles of building a consulting business and for endlessly encouraging me in my professional growth. To George Morrisey, my lasting gratitude for graciously sharing your wisdom and for serving as a role model of professional excellence. To Dr. Randy Capps, thank you for showing me the path to a glorious lifetime of studying, teaching, and learning. To Dr. Larry Doll, thanks for offering me a first taste of corporate America. And to Dr. Tom Abbott, a counselor, teacher, friend, and confidant, I shall always cherish our many conversations on life, love, and balancing the departmental budgets.

To my lifelong friends Tom Dressler, Gene Stern, Kevin Stephens, Bill Silberman, Rose Travis, and Jim Blair, thank you for helping me to keep my perspective. To my "roomie" Jack

Wilner and my kindred spirit Margot Robinson, your friendships inspire my heart and delight my soul.

Finally, this book would be incomplete without one very special acknowledgment. Thank you, Reverend Kit Carson Yeaste, for your guidance in my spiritual growth.

Introduction

"Society is always taken by surprise at any new example of common sense."

—Ralph Waldo Emerson

All authors attempt to make their books different. Obviously, I believe that to be true about this book. Here is why.

First, it is not a "cookbook," some chronological step-by-step instruction manual on how to create the "perfect" company. There is no perfect company, and probably never will be. It is rather a blueprint that offers a solid model backed by dozens of bite-sized, commonsense best practices from leading companies all over the world on how to create a high-energy workplace. I have attempted to uncover and share practical, innovative, yet realistic people practices that have already proven successful within some of today's most pioneering organizations.

Second, this book is not about how to build a "club-house" for employees, a utopian work environment of endless pampering or self-indulgence. No such successful business exists. The aim of any capitalistic business is profit, but our relentless pursuit of profit has recently taken an ugly turn. A driving force behind this book is what many senior (fifty-year-old+) executives have confided to me over the past few years—that today's business environment is the most "cutthroat," "profit-centered," and "heartless" they have ever witnessed (their words, not mine). The truth, they say, is that behind the glowing press releases and the wall-mounted values statements proclaiming "our people are our greatest asset," most corporate decisions today are made with little or no regard for their human impact, the impact upon the very group companies so often label their "greatest asset."

This book, in contrast, focuses on how to build a "lighthouse," a beacon of organizational excellence that attracts and retains the best, the brightest, and the most talented employees available. It's not based on sugarcoated, goody-two-shoes hype, but on how tough, profitable companies have become the "employers of choice" in their industries through balancing their strategic business plans (for profits) with an equally powerful strategic people plan (for the profit makers).

Third, I do not intend to suggest here that all organizations must act and be alike. To the contrary, I hope this book illustrates the bountiful diversity through which great companies build powerful relationships with their employees.

Fourth, this book is not THE FINAL WORD on generating an environment of excellence at work. It is my best attempt to summarize what I have learned from years of corporate and operations management, research, reading, company visits, questioning, probing, stumbling, and agonizing over what organizations can do to maintain the towering levels of employee commitment necessary for them to thrive in our "incredibly bonkers" world (thanks, Tom Peters, for this wonderful expression).

Fifth, this book is not about products or distribution or marketing or strategic positioning, or even about systems or technology or processes. This book is about *people*—people like you and me who care about the quality of their work and the quality of their workplace. Anita Roddick, the founder of The Body Shop, believes that "people, rather than things, will be the focus of business in the future." She is absolutely right, and that focus has already begun.

Finally, this book is not a destination but rather a starting point from which you can help release the natural energy, drive, enthusiasm, and motivation that already exist within your employees. For a few, this book represents a simple reformation or reinforcement of things you currently do. But for many this book represents a transformation in thinking and a radical departure from current attempts to revitalize employee commitment. Whether a reformation or a transformation, my hope is that the discussions and action ideas presented here will inspire you to create an action plan that will tap your company's only true competitive advantage— the passionate results-focused commitment of your people!

From Dream Careers to Extreme Careers: The New Workplace Realities

"Toto, I have a feeling we are not in Kansas anymore."

—Dorothy, in *The Wizard of Oz*

Answer these three questions:

1. Over the past few years, have you found it tougher to recruit wildly enthusiastic applicants who would love an opportunity to work for your company?
2. Over the past few years, have you found it more difficult than ever to keep employee motivation high?
3. Over the past few years, have you found that you can no longer expect unconditional commitment and loyalty from your employees?

If you are anything like the vast majority of managers and supervisors across America, your answer to all three questions is a resounding yes! It is tougher than ever to recruit, motivate, and inspire the commitment of employees today. We can no longer expect an endless line of enthusiastic jobs applicants fighting one another to join our companies. We can no longer expect that traditional motivational techniques will have any lasting impact. We can no longer expect the unconditional commitment and loyalty of any employee.

Just like countless colleagues, you are probably asking yourself, "Hey, what's going on around here? Why is it more difficult today to surround myself with enthusiastic, motivated, and committed employees?" The answer is quite simple. The rules have changed! The workplace realities of yesterday no longer exist. What was once our dream of a lifetime job guarantee in exchange for a lifetime of company loyalty has died. Our "dream careers" have been transformed into "extreme careers" in which the only guarantee is that there are no guarantees.

The new workplace realities have radically changed the way employees view the role of work within their lives. No longer do employees believe in the work covenants of the past. They recognize the new realities and have adjusted their thinking accordingly. However, most companies continue to operate under the old workplace realities and have failed to adjust their thinking or their operations. Just as the workplace rules have forever changed, so too must the way companies meet the new motivational needs of today's employee. To meet the new challenges, we must first understand how the dream careers of yesterday have been transformed into the extreme careers of today.

The Birth of the Dream Career

The dream was born in the middle of the twentieth century. Living through depressions and two world wars, our parents and grandparents forged an economy that fulfilled the career dream of every worker—a lifetime job for a lifetime of work. An unofficial motto for the dream career could have been WORK HARD, LIFE IS TOUGH. Through their hard work, markets grew, products were in demand, and lifetime jobs were created.

The best companies attracted hordes of ready, willing, and able applicants fighting to get into the ranks. Our primary goal was to join a good company and let it teach us a lifetime job skill. People who came to the company with a college degree were often placed on the management fast track, a sure path to a lifetime of opportunity. Companies could sit back and play the role of judge, deciding whom they wished to grace with membership in their factory, steel mill, or office. The company held all the cards, and the job candidates knew it. But that was OK, because the dream career was based on the knowledge that the company would take care of you.

The highest praise was to be called a "company man." For the company man, the job and the career always came first. Whatever the company asked, from working late to moving across the country or around the world, the company man would oblige. Even during the 1980s, insiders at IBM, who could expect to relocate every eighteen to twenty-four months, joked that the company initials were actually an acronym for *"I've Been Moved."*

The good company man enthusiastically obeyed orders. Just like the good soldiers they were trained to be during this century's many wars, employees seldom questioned authority. For the most part, their "salute and execute" approach blended well with what most companies considered to be teamwork. From dressing alike to talking and acting alike, teamwork was stepping in line with the company line, everyone marching to the same beat.

The dream career required that all family troubles be left at home. "Don't bring your family problems to work" was a common rule. Family life was an insignificant annoyance that was not supposed to interfere with work life. Employees kept their family problems to themselves, separate from work.

Dream career loyalty was measured in years of service. A fundamental premise was the "one company, one career" philosophy. Most of our colleagues were long-term company veterans, "lifers," who stood by the company through thick and thin. In return, the company stood by them through thick and thin. For the most part, layoffs were temporary glitches, a rare bump along the dream career road.

About the worst thing that could happen in a dream career was to be asked to "step aside" and take a lesser position or a new assignment in another department. That often indicated that you would go no further up the ladder, and signaled that it was now time to ride out your employment until retirement. Anyone who was actually fired had to be either a troublemaker, a thief, or a genuinely rotten egg.

Even though senior managers in these dream careers seldom appeared in the trenches, you believed that they had your best interests in mind. You trusted them to do what was right for the long-term stability of the company and in turn for the long-term employment stability of all workers. Because of the many layers of management, it was an exciting experience to actually see or talk to the CEO, whom you held in awe.

The dream career track was obvious and attainable. Ample opportunities for advancement awaited star performers. Outstanding performance was rewarded with promotions, bigger staffs, better territories, bigger expense accounts, and even country club memberships.

The ultimate payoff for a lifetime of hard work and loyalty to the company was a guaranteed job until retirement. Work hard until you turn sixty-two or sixty-five, receive a gold watch at the retirement dinner, and take off for the trip of a lifetime. Retirement was indeed the good life. Comfort and security were guaranteed in your golden years for a lifetime of service.

Maintaining the Dream

How did companies keep the dream alive? What did they do to keep employees loyal, productive, and motivated throughout their careers?

The fundamental approach was the carrot and the stick. The carrot was the possibility of lifetime job security, including a progressive career path up the organizational ladder, annual raises, and a retirement plan. Occasionally a new title, a bigger office, and a bigger staff encouraged higher performance. The stick was the threat of taking all these away. For employees who had lived through the Great Depression and several foreign wars, the threat of losing pension, seniority, and security was often enough to get them to straighten up and tow the company line. Hence, the "you're lucky just to have a job" approach to supervision was common.

Employee recognition consisted mostly of handing out occasional certificates or awards, distributing turkeys at Thanksgiving, and a promise of more work to come. Being invited to a training seminar, even one sponsored by the company, was an early indication of either a promotion or a forthcoming job assignment. A promotion to headquarters was considered a move to Mecca; you had arrived!

Employees were encouraged to spend time together outside of work. Companies sponsored softball, baseball, and bowling leagues, held annual picnics, and organized anything that would get employees to spend even more time together.

The annual managers' meetings featured plenty of food, drink, and "rah-rah" motivational speakers. And it worked. All employees needed was just an occasional break with a quick booster shot of inspiration to remind them of how good it was to work for the company.

That's basically how we approached maintaining high motivation within the dream career. A few carrots and sticks, an occasional gift, continual promises of more work, chances to socialize with other company employees, promotional opportunities, and an injection of some inspirational happy talk were typical approaches to getting employees to stay committed, loyal, and productive. That worked then, but times have changed.

The Death of the Dream Career

Perhaps the most important series of events in American business history occurred in the early 1990s. Throughout the endless announcements of thousands upon thousands of jobs being lost, we continued to hope that somewhere there were companies that would be immune. We looked to the last heroes of dream careers, gallant companies that would maintain the ultimate core covenant between an employer and its employees: Work hard, apply your craft, and we (the company) will take care of you during your work years and beyond. But with a combination of sadness and genuine remorse, the last holdouts of lifetime job guarantees, progressive companies including IBM and Apple Computer, announced their first-ever layoffs. The dream career had died.

The Birth of the Extreme Career

The death of lifetime job security has forever changed the way employees view the role of work in their lives. The cornerstones of the dream career—a lifetime job guarantee with full retirement benefits in exchange for a lifetime of loyalty to the company—are gone. Job security is now the ultimate oxymoron. Even the most loyal and committed employees understand that their jobs will never again be secure, that a lifetime with any company is extremely rare. For example, according to Richard Belous, chief economist of the National Planning Association, 45 million people today are either self-employed or working as temps, part-timers, or consultants.[1] That is fully one-third of the American working population. In Europe, the figure is already close to 50 percent.[2]

Good-bye, dream careers. We loved you and hoped you'd never go away. Rest in peace.

Hello, extreme careers. We may not love you, but we know you're here to stay.

The New Guarantee

At the core of the extreme career is the frightening realization that the only guarantee at work is that there is no guarantee—none, zero, zilch. Markets, even entire industries, can disappear overnight. Steady employment has never been more precarious. William Morin, chairman of the outplacement firm Drake, Beam, Morin, believes that of the eight jobs Americans can expect to hold during their working years, four will terminate involuntarily. Further, he contends that "companies no longer offer people careers . . . people create their own careers."[3]

The uncertainties of extreme careers cause people to wonder if today might be their last day with the company. Instead of working under the security blanket of a lifetime job, employees consistently question whether they might get outplaced, downsized, rightsized, reengineered, or see the company bought, sold, merged, or purged. This uneasiness permeates all levels of organizations.

The New Loyalty

In dream careers, loyalty was measured by years with one company. In extreme careers, loyalty is measured in months and has nothing to do with a one-career, one-company philosophy. Today it's not *if* we should begin our second career but rather *when* to begin our second, third, or even fourth career, regardless of our current employer. Employees today are more loyal to themselves than to their employers. Goran Lindahl, a group executive vice president for the successful international power-equipment company ABB Asea Brown Boveri, told the *Harvard Business Review* that "managers are loyal not to a particular boss or even to a company but to a set of values they believe in and find satisfying."[4] This new philosophy implies that employees keep one foot in the door until something better comes along.

The New Motivators for Extreme Careers

With such instability and uncertainty, today's employees have changed their motivations to fit their new realities. A new order has emerged in the value systems of employees. Instead of the dream career motto of WORK HARD, LIFE IS TOUGH, the unofficial motto of extreme careers might well be PLAY HARD, LIFE IS SHORT. Personal fulfillment is becoming more important than personal wealth, particularly for baby busters, those people born between 1965 and 1983. Busters are the first generation in this century to believe that their future will not exceed or even equal that of their parents. So it is easy to understand why two-thirds of busters believe that the purpose in life is enjoyment and personal fulfillment.[5]

Faced with the prospect of lifelong job uncertainty and insecurity, employees today are searching for opportunities that engage their spirits, ignite their souls, and balance their lives. Putting the career first while robustly pursuing the bottom line has been replaced by putting the family first while robustly pursuing a better quality of life. A revealing example of this new focus is the 1994 graduating class of the Harvard Business School, which ranked money only seventh on a list of what was most important in considering a new position. Things like span of responsibility and corporate culture ranked higher. The extreme career company man or woman will more quickly question the transfer or promotion than the dream career company employee ever did. They will ask themselves: "How will it affect the family?" "Do I want to uproot the kids?" "What is the backup if we move and the company is then bought, sold, merged, or purged?" We all know colleagues who have refused to take a new job or to be transferred out of state because of the potential disruption to their personal lives.

Employees today demand that their jobs be at the very least interesting and challenging. The rationale is simple— why keep a routine, boring job that offers no job security? An even worse scenario for many of our best employees is to get caught within an uptight, overly serious workplace that forbids people to celebrate or have fun. Extreme careers are tough enough. But when companies refuse to allow employees to occasionally lighten up and have some fun, the best employees will leave while those that remain slowly lose their spirit, zest, and enthusiasm for their work.

Climbing the corporate ladder has been replaced by scaling the corporate step stool for extreme career employees. The few remaining management layers left are typically clogged with baby boomers. With no upward advancement in sight, employees are demanding more direct involvement in decision making, greater personal input in policy, and more autonomy in their work. Further, with no job certainty, employees demand to be kept informed about what is happening in the company. The rationale is simple. If you cannot promise me a job, much less an upward career track, the least you can do is to keep me informed about company plans so I can help myself. It's really a "I want to help you help me stay employed" approach.

The paternalistic model of employment no longer exists. Employees rationalize that if a company can no longer treat them as family, then at least it ought to treat them as business partners. Forget fancy titles and big offices. Extreme career employees want a piece of the business, a stake in its success. Status and power are not as important as sharing and caring. For employees, the paternalistic dream career approach was "What can you do for me tomorrow?" The extreme career approach is "What have you done for me lately?"

A college degree is no longer a guarantee of a fast-track career. With the incredible pace of change, technological advance, and information growth, extreme careers are built upon continual learning. The knowledge acquired in college becomes outdated in a few years. Extreme careers offer the choice of either keeping up or falling behind. Training is no longer a "nice to have" extra but an absolute competitive necessity for survival.

A final key motivator within today's extreme career is freedom. More than ever before, employees demand greater independence, autonomy, and freedom from bureaucracy. Countless books and magazine articles report the hordes of great managers leaving corporate America. They are tired of feeling fenced in by endless policies and procedures. They are exhausted from playing corporate politics. Frustrated by years of asking someone else for permission to act, many of today's best employees refuse to play the losing game of corporate survival, which only increases their chance of being outplaced during next year's company downsizing.

Getting Employees to Fall in Love With Our Companies

Now you know why it is harder to find wildly enthusiastic applicants and tougher to motivate employees, and why we can no longer count on unconditional employee commitment or loyalty. Now try to imagine that as you drive by your work site tomorrow, you see every off-duty salaried employee washing and cleaning your company's facilities. Just imagine that if your employees are given the opportunity to either keep their incentive bonuses or to give them back to the company to help pay down corporate debt, they choose to help pay down corporate debt! Now imagine that when you call your nonmandatory quarterly employee meeting at its normal time of 6:00 A.M.—on Sunday morning—95 percent of the employees show up!

Do these scenarios sound like fantasies concocted by the imagination of a business consultant or fiction writer? Could such fantastic events occur today? Both on and off-duty pilots at Southwest Airlines are often found voluntarily washing and cleaning their airplanes. The employees of Springfield ReManufacturing recently gave back their bonuses to the company to help pay down corporate debt. The quarterly employee meetings at The Home Depot attract hordes of enthusiastic employees that turn the early Sunday morning, live interactive, satellite-uplink gatherings into celebrations.

Would you say that the employees at companies like Southwest Airlines, Springfield ReManufacturing, and The Home Depot are more than just warm bodies who show up for their shift? Would you say that employees who voluntarily clean their environments, give back their bonuses, and meet on early Sunday mornings more than just *like* their companies? Dare we even imply in these cynical 1990s that these employees may actually *love* what they do and who they are doing it for? Most important, would you say that because of their incredibly high levels of employee commitment that these companies have a *distinct competitive advantage* in their marketplace?

This book will show you how companies like Southwest Airlines, Springfield ReManufacturing, The Home Depot, and dozens more like them generate phenomenal levels of employee commitment, productivity, and even love. It presents five key principles, supported by dozens of easy-to-duplicate, successful "best practices," used by progressive companies of all sizes and kinds, that can inspire the bottom-line results-focused commitment of all employees. The principles and examples that follow will enable you to:

1. Capture the hearts and minds of all your employees.
2. Open communication between all levels of your organization.
3. Create partnerships between all employees built upon trust, equality, and sharing.
4. Drive learning into every nook and cranny of your company.
5. Emancipate the action of every employee to increase service and profits.

Capture the Heart: Unleash the Joy

"The highest achievable level of service comes from
the heart, so the company that reaches its people's
heart will provide the very best service."

—Hal Rosenbluth, CEO, Rosenbluth Travel

Is excellence possible with a disengaged heart?

Reflect for a moment on your most significant accomplishments. Do they include reaching an incredibly tough work or professional goal? Raising a fine daughter or son? Perhaps building that special house or catching a record-breaking fish? To succeed in any worthwhile endeavor, it takes effort, focus, and time. Yet within every success lies a common thread, a special something that sparks our commitment to excellence. What is it? What is that special element that ignites us to excel?

Regardless of the endeavor, whether at work, at home, or at play, excellence is only possible with an actively engaged heart. When something captures your heart, you are driven to succeed, to complete that project or catch that fish. Imagine attempting to accomplish anything important in your life when the activity does not engage your heart. If your heart is not in the task, can you automatically give it 100 percent of your effort? Will you go the extra mile to be successful if the activity does not somehow touch your heart?

At the heart of the matter, then, is the heart, for without an actively engaged heart, excellence is impossible.

Doin' Time

You can see them in every industry almost anywhere you go—employees going through the motions of their jobs, exerting just enough effort to reach the minimum standards of acceptable job performance. It's the retail clerk who regimentally mumbles "Can I help you?" It's the factory worker or the office supervisor who says she's just "putting in my hours to go home." It's a colleague who constantly watches the clock, ready to bolt out the door at quitting time. Ever wonder what these people do away from work? Do you think they approach their personal lives in the same way they approach their work lives? *No way!* Away from work, these very same people, these graduates of "Warm Body University," are incredibly active and committed. They build furniture and lead youth and church groups. They head civic organizations and go on family camping and fishing trips. They read books and take college and extension courses to improve themselves. They repair cars, play golf, run 5-K's, and shoot basketball. They attend football games and parades and rock concerts. They organize cookouts and fund-raisers and birthday bashes.

Our employees are dedicated, energetic, motivated, caring people, always bettering themselves and bettering the world around them—until they show up for work! Why is that? Could it be that all the stuff outside of work engages their hearts more than all the stuff inside of work?

Heartpower

Speaking to the American Management Association shortly before his death, the legendary coach of the Green Bay Packers, Vince Lombardi, said that "Heartpower is the strength of your corporation." He's right. Look behind any of your company's greatest accomplishments and you will find that its driving force was not necessarily a brilliantly conceived strategy (although that helps) or a seamlessly executed plan (that would be a miracle). The driving force behind all great organizational achievements is the heartpower of the employees, their engaged passion for excellence.

Heartpower may be the most underutilized resource in business today. It's a limitless resource available to every company, yet few companies take advantage of it. Every day millions of employees filled with untapped heartpower go to work, where they wait for their organizations to give them a reason to commit themselves, a reason to exert their energies, a reason to excel. Unfortunately, most managers choose to ignore this untapped resource. They prefer to hide behind the "bottom line" and to manage people on the sole basis of the hard, cold numbers of the business. In doing so, they fail to capitalize on the single greatest motivator of them all.

Companies that capture the hearts of their employees seldom need to worry about motivation. Engaged hearts motivate themselves. Engaged hearts experience the excitement of a challenge, the thrill of competition, and the joy of success. As Yvon Chouinard, the founder of Patagonia, says, "You don't need to manage self-motivated people, and nearly everyone is motivated when they are doing a job they believe in."

Heartpower is the very core of any successful enterprise. Capture the heart, and you have captured the employee. For without a vibrant, beating heart, any enterprise is sure to die. Today's great managers capture the hearts of their employees through focusing on three strategies:

1. Live a compelling vision.
2. Balance work and family.
3. Celebrate and have fun.

Live a Compelling Vision

We have heard it before, things like, "All we need is a vision and a mission statement—that will solve our problems." So we hire expensive consultants to create gloriously worded sentiments that are engraved on fancy wall plaques and pocket cards only to discover that nothing really changes. Cynics scoff at such undertakings, believing that the creation of a vision or mission statement is a waste of time and energy. They miss the underlying reasons why we humans desire such statements. An inscription on a church wall in the county of Sussex, England, reminds us why such proclamations are vital. It reads:

> A task without a vision is drudgery.
> A vision without a task is but a dream.
> But a vision with a task is the hope of the world.

Do you ever wonder how many people wake up and march to the factory or the office or the store thinking that their work is drudgery. More than we would probably care to admit. Yet organizations continue to dump more and more drudgery on their employees without a compelling set of guiding principles to engage their hearts (tasks without a vision). Some offer a grand plan, but offer no guidelines on how to achieve it (vision without a task). It is the same thing as a parent who says to her child, "Do your homework—do your homework" (task without a vision) or "Become your best—become your best" (vision without a task), versus the parent who says to her child, "Become your best through learning your lessons" (task with a vision). Which child do you think is more likely to reach excellence?

The world is filled with examples of compelling visions. Fed Ex's is simply PEOPLE—SERVICE—PROFITS. Southwest Airlines' unofficial vision is to HAVE FUN AND MAKE A PROFIT. Ford Motors' says QUALITY IS JOB ONE. The vision of the Wisconsin sausage maker Johnsonville Foods is WE SELL GREAT TASTE AND FUN. ServiceMaster's is HONORING GOD IN ALL WE DO. The movie *Field of Dreams* beautifully illustrates the blinding commitment generated by a compelling vision in the simple phrase "Build it and he will come."

However, beware the false vision. A heart-filled vision is much more than a financial goal or a well-thought-out strategic plan. As Bill Wiggenhorn, President of Motorola University, reminds us (and this may come as a shock to many financial managers), the so-called vision of "Shareholder Equity, Rah! Rah! Rah! just doesn't get people out of bed each day." When Dr. Martin Luther King, Jr., spoke to 500,000 civil rights marchers in front of the Lincoln Memorial, he did not exclaim, "I have a *strategic plan* today." Dr. King knew that strategic plans do not stir the soul, do not enliven the spirit, do not capture the heart. So, Dr. King, understanding the power of a compelling vision, enthusiastically proclaimed "I have a *dream* today," which became the focus of the entire civil rights movement.

To capture the hearts of our employees, it is essential that we tell them what we stand for and where we are going. Our vision must be compelling, understandable, and focused. It must not be a graduate diatribe on some esoteric philosophy or financial position. And it must be wholehearted, not a half-hearted attempt to artificially arouse passions. Perhaps the best explanation as to why a compelling vision is so important can be found in Proverbs 29:18, which reads, "Where there is no vision, the people perish."

Balance Work and Family

One of today's great challenges is finding a reasonable balance between our work and our personal lives. With the tremendous competitive pressures of the marketplace, companies demand more and more of our time and efforts. In so doing, they place ever increasing pressure on us to attempt to balance the legitimate needs of our employers with the legitimate desire to have a life outside of work. However, we are not the first generation to experience these pressures.

In the fall of 1963, my father moved our family to Bardstown, Kentucky, a small town south of Louisville. It happened to be our fourth move in eight years—all dictated by my father's employer, a regional finance company. He usually traveled five to six days a week for the company, and as a result, my early memories of my father are rather vague. After this move, however, he stayed home, working out of a home office, building a successful real estate and insurance business. Being all of ten years old, I was not sure why this was happening, but I was sure enjoying playing baseball and spending more time with him.

Several years later, I asked him why we had moved to this small town and why he decided to work for himself. He told me, "Jim, I had three kids I barely knew and a wife I wanted to know even better. I was tired of traveling and being told by someone else what to do and where to go. There's never been anything more important to me than you, your brother and sister, and your mom. So, I decided that, whatever the price, I was going to find a way to be with all of you. I was not going to let you grow up without me." Like so many people today, my father was driven to find a good balance between his professional life and his personal life, regardless of the price.

When companies neglect to help their employees better balance the demands of work with the need for a personal life, they risk burning out or even losing their best talent. It is not just the front line or middle management that feels this pressure. Even top management feels the heat. A 1994 survey by management consultants at Robert Half International found that 91 percent of executives take work home at least several times a week. They warned top management to "better balance their work and personal lives" or "risk losing top people to burnout."

Without a concerted effort to balance work and life demands, employers could succumb to what the Japanese call *karoshi,* or death by overwork. Sadly, it is not unusual to find a Japanese worker slumped over his work area, dead, literally having died from overwork. Fortunately, more and more top American executives are speaking out on this vital issue. Jack Welch, CEO of General Electric, is often quoted as saying, "If someone tells me they're working 90 hour weeks, I tell them they're doing something terribly wrong." Jim Ivey, CEO of Barnett Bank of Tampa, recently said, "This [helping employees balance work and family life] is very bottom-line oriented. The days of bragging about 80-hour workweeks are over. There is life outside banking."

To capture the hearts of today's employees, managers must take a positive approach to balancing work and life and not mimic the approach taken by the Houston Oilers professional football team toward one of its star players. During the 1993 NFL football season, offensive tackle David Williams chose to miss a game to stay with his wife during childbirth. The Oilers fined him $125,000.

According to Ann McGee-Cooper, author of *You Don't Have to Go Home From Work Exhausted*, the single greatest element of high-energy living is balance; the greater the balance, the greater the energy, joy, enthusiasm, and creativity.[1] It's just like the old expression "All work and no play makes Jack a dull fellow and Jill a rich widow." Think about your positive work/life balance this way. You would never exclaim with your last breath, "You know, I wish I had spent more time at the office!"

Celebrate and Have Fun

When Ben and Jerry's Homemade announced their "Yo, We Want You To Be Our CEO" contest, some 20,000 ice cream fanatics applied, including me. Although it was a shock not to have been offered an interview, the greatest shock occurred when I opened the large envelope with postage stamped from Waterbury, Vermont. Enclosed was an $8^1/2'' \times 11''$ *Official Rejection Letter*—suitable for framing! This multicolored certificate had a picture of Ben Cohen and Jerry Greenfield, side by side, each wearing a huge top hat emblazoned with the logo of their favorite Ben & Jerry's flavor (White Russian and Chocolate Chip Cookie respectively, in case you wanted to know). With the caption, "We almost wanted you, Jim Harris, to be our CEO," this *Official Rejection Letter* goes on to say that "it warms our hearts—and blows our minds—that someone of your high caliber would even *consider* a career with us. Your talents and potential convinced us that a much higher calling awaits you. You're just too valuable to the world to be peddling ice cream. Be happy, go lucky." But there was more.

[1]Ann McGee-Cooper, *You Don't Have to Go Home From Work Exhausted* (Dallas: Bowen and Rogers, 1990), p. 17.

Also in the rejection envelope was a coupon for a free pint of Ben & Jerry's ice cream (my favorite is Chunky Monkey, in case you wanted to know). And there was even more. They also included a "Call for Kids" brochure that discussed several worthwhile children's agencies that do good work in Vermont, with an encouragement to contact your local agencies to volunteer.

After laughing out loud at the colorful, outlandish, and brilliantly conceived certificate, and quickly deciding at which store to redeem my coupon, I glanced through the "Call for Kids" information—and it hit me. If this is how they treat their rejected applicants, imagine how well they treat their employees! If I was indeed serious about wanting to go to work there, this rejection packet would have redoubled my efforts to join them—in any capacity! With one incredibly fun, insightful, and meaningful mailing, Ben & Jerry's Homemade created both an admirer and a customer for life. Imagine being associated with a company that projects a spirit of celebration and fun that even rejected applicants can participate in!

How can managers ever expect us to fall in love with a company that is boring, stoic, and staid? How can we ever put our whole hearts into an organization that does not allow for a spirit of joyous, uplifting celebration? Why do so many managers lack the foresight to see the effects of celebration and positive fun on the spirit and productivity of the workplace? When asked where he would go to work if he were to start over again, Microsoft founder Bill Gates did not mention any industry or profession; rather, he discussed the importance of making work both fun and interesting. Occasionally, we need to remind each other of what the famous defense lawyer Clarence Darrow once said: "If you lose the power to laugh, you lose the power to think."

To attract and retain today's best and brightest employees, and to inspire excellence in them, great companies invigorate their workplaces with uplifting, fun-drenched activities. May we all leave our work legacy in the same manner as Malcolm Forbes, the founder of *Forbes* magazine, who left this world with a tombstone that reads, "While alive, he lived."

Best Practices

Here are thirty-five examples of how companies capture the hearts of their employees.

1. "WHAT KIND OF COMPANY?"

When General Motors formed its Saturn Corporation, the key question was not what kind of car to make but rather "What kind of company do you want to work for?" This is a core question to consider when you want to capture the hearts of employees, and can easily serve as the basis for an employee meeting on creating a company vision.

2. "BECOME THE BEST."

The Ritz-Carlton Hotel Company is the first service company to win the coveted Malcolm Baldrige award for quality. One of the key reasons it earned this honor was that CEO Horst Schulze successfully drove his passionate vision of world-class guest service throughout the chain. Whenever he meets with staff, especially during a grand opening before the employees have worked their first day, Schulze will ask every employee in all departments two questions: "In six months, what do *you* want to become?" and "In six months, what do you want *your department* to become?" Across all cultures from around the world, Schulze has found that people answer both questions exactly the same way—"to become the *best!*" Schulze's simple questions keep the commitment to excellence alive throughout the Ritz-Carlton.

3. "COOL VISION."

Galacticomm, the Fort Lauderdale software developer, firmly believes that you do not need to hire consultants or form executive committees to create a powerful vision. What is its vision? "To do really cool things in the field of computer communications and make a buck at it."

4. "WE CREATE HAPPINESS."

Ask any of the 36,000 Walt Disney World cast members (employees) to recite the Disney Corporation's service vision and they will tell you, "We create happiness by providing the finest in entertainment to people of all ages, everywhere." Even if they only remember the first three words, "We create happiness," the message is clear. When was the last time you asked your colleagues to recite your vision or mission? If you have one, do you know it by heart? Can you even remember the first three words?

5. "I BELIEVE."

Few things are more powerful in capturing the hearts of employees than knowing exactly what their senior managers believe in and what they stand for. When Ron Peterson called his first employee meeting as the new CEO of Florida Forest Products, a building products and specialty lumber company, he opened the meeting by discussing "Twelve Things I Believe In." His list included a belief in fairness, integrity, caring, sharing, and earning an honest profit. Ron laid the foundation for the new culture through his powerful, personal message of what he believed in.

6. "DUAL MISSIONS."

Bread Loaf Construction has a unique way of gaining a two-way buy-in from its employees. It offers programs to its employees on how to build *personal* mission statements. Discussions with each employee help integrate their personal missions with the company mission, thereby making Bread Loaf a company in which all employees can reach their personal goals. These dual missions create a positive, two-way buy-in for the employee and for the company.

7. "WE WILL."

Capturing the hearts of employees is particularly critical during mergers or acquisitions. When AT&T acquired McCaw Cellular Communications, all McCaw employees received a packet that included coupons for AT&T discounts, a pamphlet of handwritten greetings from AT&T employees, the AT&T mission statement, a welcome video from AT&T executives, and a poster and T-shirt emblazoned with the message WHO WILL LEAD THE FUTURE OF COMMUNICATIONS? WE WILL. The packet also included a sheet of "We Will" stickers.

8. "CUSTOMERS, TOO."

At companies like Haworth, Inc., the office furniture manufacturer, and Sewell Motor Company, the automobile dealership, presentations are given to customers on the company's mission. Potential customers at Haworth hear executives discuss the company's mission and its importance to the organization. At Sewell Motors, potential customers view a video on what it's like to become a member of the Sewell automotive family.

9. "CHARITY DAY."

Recognizing how difficult it can be to find time for volunteer work with favorite charities, McCormick & Company, the Baltimore spice manufacturer, opens its plants one Saturday every year for what it calls "Charity Day." Employees *voluntarily* work their normal shifts for no pay. For volunteering, McCormick donates double the employee's daily wage to the charity of the employee's choice. This is a true win-win-win situation. The employees win through earning money for their favorite charities, the charities win through the donations received, and McCormick wins the goodwill of the community as well as gaining a day of production.

10. "SOS."

ARES, Inc., the commercial office building property management group, has taken the concept of balancing work and life to its customers. Their SOS (*Services On the Spot*) program offers tenants the ability to run "errands at your desk," including auto tag and title renewal, on-site automobile oil changes and detailing, driver's license renewal through the Georgia Licenses on Wheels ("GLOW") mobile service, shoe repair, dry cleaning, and drugstore items delivery.

11. "DROP IT OFF."

Large for-profit businesses by no means have an exclusive on helping employees balance work and family life. The Pinellas County, Florida, Public School Administrative offices offer a small area in which employees can drop off clothing needing dry cleaning in the morning so that a local dry cleaner can pick them up and return the clothes by the end of the workday. This is a simple, effective time-saver for the administrative staff.

12. "KIDS & GRAMPS."

More and more companies recognize the increasing demands on some employees to provide both child and adult care. Progressive companies such as Lancaster Laboratories, the Pennsylvania manufacturer, and Stride Rite, the California shoe maker, offer both subsidized on-site child care and adult care facilities. Imagine a company that cares so much for its employees that it creates an opportunity for three generations of a family to lunch together on company grounds! Would that capture your heart? Stride Rite is so committed to such quality of work-life issues that it insisted that a new venture partner in Thailand open a day care center for its employees.

13. "MORE TEA, MOM?"

Recognizing the new pressures that the necessity for finding elder care places on many employees, companies like First National Bank of Maryland allow employees occasionally to bring their parents to the office.

14. "TEACH YOUR CHILDREN WELL."

The John Nuveen Co., a Chicago-based financial services group, and Eaton Corporation, the Cleveland-based truck parts and electrical power distribution manufacturer, take teaching children to a new level. Nuveen offers to pay the college tuition of children of full-time employees with five or more years' service. As CEO Richard Franke says, "If we take away the worry of paying for college, employees will concentrate more and be more productive. We value our employees, and this is a great way to keep them." There may be no better way to walk the talk of the value of both family and education than through Nuveen's progressive example. Eaton matches, on a dollar-for-dollar basis, education costs up to $5,000 a year per employee from kindergarten through graduate school.

15. "No Sundays."

Since founding his company in 1946, S. Truett Cathy has never allowed his Chick-fil-A restaurants to open on Sundays. He believes it is hypocritical to have "my cash register jingling" while professing the Sabbath as holy. Whether you agree with Cathy or not, employees are inspired when they see their leaders walk their talk.

16. "Plane Names."

A great way to capture the hearts of employees is to focus on the employee's family. Federal Express now names its planes after the children of employees. It also flies the entire family to see the plane when it is christened.

17. "Core Hours."

Meredith Publishing employs a sensible, adult approach to helping employees balance work and personal life. All employees must work the "core hours" between 10:00 A.M. and 3:00 P.M. This gives them the leeway to come in as late as 10:00 A.M. and work until 6:00 P.M., or to come in as early as 6:00 A.M. and work until 3:00 P.M. It's an easy, effective way to treat employees as adults by allowing them the freedom to decide which hours are most convenient.

18. "SCHOOL BUSINESS."

Ridgeview Hosiery, the North Carolina manufacturer, understands the pressure on working parents to keep up with their children's progress in school. So, it arranges for school counselors to meet on-site with parents during regular working hours. Going one step further, the Charlotte-based NationsBank encourages all employees to spend up to two paid hours per week helping community schools.

19. "BABY BEEPERS."

First Interstate Bank of California in Los Angeles offers free beepers to employees so spouses can keep in touch during the last months of a woman's pregnancy. The bank also lends out electric breast-pump machines so that mothers do not have to choose between returning to work and continuing their breast feeding.

20. "HANDY MAN."

Wilton Conner Packaging, the North Carolina manufacturer, has on its payroll an experienced maintenance worker whom employees can hire to do everything from painting their house to unclogging drains and even building room additions—simply for the cost of supplies! It also provides a "Buck a Load" clothes service, where for $1 a load, employees can drop off their laundry and get it washed, dried, and folded. Ironing costs an extra 25¢ per item!

21. "FLOWER POWER."

The headquarters of Delta Airlines sends flowers to employees who are ill or have a death in the family. Once a year, all employees of Townsend Engineering, the Des Moines, Iowa, meat-processing equipment manufacturer, may send up to $50 worth of flowers to a friend or loved one—at company expense!

22. "CHILDREN, BEHAVE!"

Prospect Associates, a health research and communications company in Rockville, Maryland, has a long-standing policy of allowing employees to bring their children to work as long as they are well behaved and do not disturb operations. On the first day, Prudential Insurance offered its employees a free videotape on how to positively discipline kids; over 11,000 of Prudential's 99,000 employees called to request a copy.

23. "WEEKEND WARRIORS."

Rodale Press, the Emmaus, Pennsylvania, publisher, encourages balancing work and life by renting to employees high-quality athletic and camping equipment. The nominal costs range from $2 for in-line skates to $10 for a complete camping package that includes a tent and sleeping bags.

24. "FOLLOW THE (FUN) RULES."

The advertising agency Dahlin Smith White injects fun and creativity into work by giving all its employees a small "art budget" with which to decorate their offices. But as they decorate they must follow the company motto, DO SOMETHING WILD! What a great way to unleash the creative juices and capture the hearts of employees!

25. "BREAK THE MONOTONY."

Having fun within a hospital setting might be considered an oxymoron, but Baptist Hospital in Miami, Florida, found a simple, effective way of doing it. On nontraditional occasions such as Oktoberfest or the birthday of a famous poet, the staff opens a small auditorium for what it calls a "Monotony Breaker Day." Snacks, drinks, and room decorations symbolize that day's theme. All employees are encouraged to drop by the room whenever it's convenient to socialize, relax, or take a break from the intense pressures and/or monotony of a hospital environment.

26. "SERIOUS FUN."

Employees at Silicon Graphics, the California software developer, have been known to break into water cannon battles to celebrate major breakthroughs or the completion of major projects. CEO Ed McCracken summarizes their mission as "serious fun." Silicon Graphics even has a line item in its budget for "morale."

27. "PET DAZE."

The headquarters of Domino's Pizza allows employees to bring their pets to work on Fridays. Employees at Open Market, the software services company, can bring their dogs to work any day of the week.

28. "ODD COUPLES."

Felix Unger (the neatness freak) and Oscar Madison (the slob) are the main characters of Neil Simon's wonderful play *The Odd Couple.* First Chicago, the bank holding company, hands out "Felix and Oscar Awards" to those employees with the neatest and messiest desks, respectively.

29. "BAG THE INTERVIEW."

Several years ago, when the office of Amy's Ice Creams in Austin, Texas, happened to run out of job application forms, it improvised by handing each applicant an empty bag with the instructions to "improvise." It worked beautifully, because Amy's hires only people who care about the job and who can entertain customers. One ingenious applicant transformed her bag into a helium-filled hot-air balloon and floated it into the interview area. The bags continue to be a standard part of the interview process.

30. "KAZOOS, NOT BOOS."

Employees at Apple Computers have been known to use kazoos instead of applause at meetings to show their approval (or disapproval) of speakers.

31. "Joy Gangs."

Jerry Greenfield, co-founder of Ben & Jerry's Homemade, is the self-proclaimed "Minister of Joy" of the "Joy Gang." The gang's sole purpose is "the relentless pursuit of joy in the workplace, leaving a trail of deliriously happy employees wherever it goes." From coordinating special celebrations such as "National Clash Dressing Day" and "Elvis Day," on which everyone is served greasy hamburgers, to cooking complete Italian meals for the third-shift workers while a disc jockey plays song requests, Greenfield and his gang are on the lookout for ways to inject a little fun into the workplace.

32. "No Ties."

To preserve the casual style of a start-up company, Salem Sportswear of Hudson, New Hampshire, posted a sign above its reception area that reads NO TIES BEYOND THIS POINT. Anyone caught wearing a tie beyond that point, including visitors, is fined $2, with the proceeds going to charity.

33. "Sick and Tired Award."

While Tom Melohn was CEO of North American Tool and Dye, the San Francisco manufacturer, he became sick and tired. That is, he became sick and tired of hearing from all his customers what an outstanding job his dye makers were doing! So he called a meeting and told everyone how sick and tired he was of hearing about their outstanding work, and then handed each of them a check for an extra week's pay. Of course, it became known as the "Sick and Tired Award."

34. "Carpet Baggers."

The headquarters of Brinker International, the Dallas-based restaurant group, holds indoor putt-putt golf tournaments. Called "carpet baggers," employees dress up, shut down the switchboard, and play a rousing nine-hole game of miniature golf.

35. "Reindeer Runs."

To bring some much needed cheer to hardworking store employees during the hectic Christmas holiday sales season, district managers at Target Department Stores conduct what they call "Reindeer Runs." These "runs" (store visits) turn into minicelebrations, with the managers giving awards to employees for outstanding work.

Action Ideas: How to Get On With It!

What can you do to capture the heart of your employee? Here are seven ideas you can run with:

1. Begin your next meeting with this question: "What kind of company do you want to work for?" Ask everyone to respond. Take careful notes, especially on the cynical comments, which often reveal some underlying obstacle to capturing the hearts of employees.

2. Open the following meeting with a ten-minute overview of what you believe in. Tie it into your summary of the notes you took at the previous meeting.

3. Have your group combine Ideas 1 and 2 and incorporate them into your own department or company vision—a simple, uncomplicated one-sentence statement that everyone believes in.

4. Assign all your employees to create their own personal mission statements. Meet with everyone to see how each individual mission ties into the larger vision, and discuss how to make both come alive. Conduct biannual checkups on both the personal missions and the group vision.

5. Ask for three volunteers to form a "Balancing Act" team. Give the team a copy of this book (or better yet, one copy per member!) and have them read this chapter (hey, why not read the whole thing?). Assign them to come up with a minimum of twenty-five ideas on how the department or company could better help employees balance work and

personal life. Act on the three most popular (and realistic) suggestions within thirty days. Act on the remaining top suggestions within sixty days.

6. Ask for three more volunteers to immediately form a "Clown Club," or "Zest Patrol," or "Celebration Station Team," or any other title that they can come up with. Give them twenty-four hours to create at least three "Fun Rules" that all department or company employees must adhere to at all times from that day forward—the group's "Holy Humor Grail," so to speak. Also give them a budget of $25 and less than one week to inject some fun, humor, zest, frivolity, zaniness, or craziness into your work area. Remind them that people are getting "Sick and Tired" of waiting to have a little fun!

7. Give office employees a noisemaker (i.e., a horn, whistle, or bell) to use on special occasions, or when they solve a problem, have thought of a great idea, or simply need a change of pace.

Open Communication: The Power of Connection

"American workers have lost the sense of security and identification with the company that gave meaning to their work lives. Now, they are searching for a connection—a commitment to something larger to replace that lost dependence on the corporation."

—*Training Magazine,* June 1993

One day a receptionist noticed a "help wanted" advertisement in her local newspaper that perfectly described her current position. Feeling a bit curious and more than a little bit anxious, she decided to confront her boss about the ad. Her boss confirmed her fears that, yes, the company was looking to replace her. So how did the receptionist respond? She took out her own ad in the same newspaper and in it proclaimed, "I quit." When asked about the receptionist's actions, her boss had the audacity to say, "Doesn't she have the courage to tell me she's quitting?"

Would you say that this boss was "connected" to this employee? Would you describe the internal relationships of this company as being built on common respect and courtesy? Do you think the boss understood or cared about the needs of the receptionist? Would the remaining employees feel highly committed to the company's success after such an incident? Could an employee ever fall in love with a company like this? Could this happen in your company?

At one time or another we have all felt disconnected from our department or our company. Disconnection hurts. It tears at the heart and dampens the spirit. It creates a sense of detachment and isolation. Disconnected employees feel left out of the information loop that is so critical to building effective relationships. As a result, employee commitment to the company decreases, cynicism and distrust rise, and organizational productivity comes to a grinding halt.

The Feeling of Connection

Think about the times you felt really connected to an organization. Remember how enthusiastic you were about being a member of the group? You felt you were an important part of the team. You jumped into major projects to which you freely contributed your time, effort, and ideas. Even in the tough times, the sense of connection helped you to recommit yourself to the company goals. You were at your best because you felt connected.

Employees long for a sense of connection to their workplace, for a relationship with their organization that represents more than just a paycheck or benefits plan. They want to feel "in the loop," plugged in to the company, with an understanding of what is happening throughout its various departments. They need to believe that they are more than just a pair of "hired hands" or a piece of machinery that can be replaced at any time. Employees long for that special sense of bonding that comes only from an environment of open communication.

How do you know when you and your organization are connecting with employees? There are some obvious signs:

1. When you connect, employees feel free to speak up. They know that their opinions matter and will get a fair hearing.
2. Connected employees are confident that they will receive timely information on things that affect both their particular area and the company at large.
3. Connection results in employee commitment, not just compliance. Unless managers actively pursue connection, their only real leverage is to rely on their authority to force employees to comply with mandates. Employees who do not feel connected to their companies seldom offer the extra energy or ideas that are so essential to succeeding in today's marketplace.
4. You are connecting when you understand the needs of your employees. Mutual understanding between employees and the company is the only way to attain the goals of high quality, great service, and a fair profit. After all, it is the employees who are responsible for generating quality, service, and profits.

High Tech and High Touch

Traditional barriers to effective organizational communication are becoming obsolete, not because of some grand corporate renaissance, but through absolute competitive necessity. Hierarchy and organizational levels of command are shrinking. Sizes of operations are also decreasing, theoretically making it easier to build connections with all employees.

Today's newest technologies, such as electronic mail and groupware communication systems, are powerful instruments in building connections between employees and the companies they work for. Such systems smash the traditional communication barriers between people of different status and location. There is no status barrier in an electronic message and there is no location barrier in sending and receiving electronic messages. The genius of global communication technologies has electronically linked us to anyone else in the world who owns a phone, a fax, or an E-mail address. Yet even with such wonderful and potentially revolutionary tools, the seemingly limitless communication options available today leave a void, a void that eats at the very soul of a corporation. Somehow, there is a missing link within all the splendor of modern communication wizardry.

Walk into any work space in America, be it a dentist's office, a supervisor's cubicle, or a repairman's garage, and you will see the human touch. It may be as simple as a picture, a child's drawing, or a special handwritten note. It might be as formal as a framed letter or as exhilarating as the personal autograph of a celebrity. One of my most prized possessions hangs in my office. It is a sheet of music with a personal message signed by my favorite musician, Jimmy Buffett. Such powerful icons represent our need for the human touch, for a human connection to our workplace. All the fancy-schmancy, newfangled electronic gee-whiz communication systems will never replace the human touch.

Building Connections

It is incredibly easy to lock ourselves in a room while electronically communicating around the world. But simply distributing more electronic mail and faxes is not enough to build connections. To build connections in today's fast-paced, "I don't have the time" world, we must never forget to complement our high-tech messages with some high-touch communication.

To build connections and to gain the commitment of their employees, companies actively employ four strategies. They:

1. Establish internal listening as a priority.
2. Use multiple internal communication channels.
3. Encourage two-way interaction.
4. Give feedback in real time.

Establish Internal Listening as a Priority

Companies today invest huge amounts of time and energy to better understand the thinking, values, and behavior patterns of their customers. Large organizations routinely spend millions of dollars on surveys, focus groups, mail-in coupons, and even interactive kiosks to help fill their craving for knowing more about their customers. What even the most well-intentioned "close to the customer" companies overlook, however, is that the very same processes they use to gain insights into their external customers could easily be used to learn more about their own employees. It's easy to overlook the men and women who actually serve and listen to our ultimate customers. No amount of sophisticated, randomly sampled customer research will ever make up for a disgruntled, disconnected frontline employee.

Few organizations today give much more than token consideration to listening to their employees. Beyond an occasional meeting or employee survey, most companies overlook the magnificent opportunities available to them to listen and learn from the very people who perform the lion's share of the real work—the frontline employees. Think about the time when you were on the front line. How often did any supervisor, manager, or (heaven help us!) senior executive actively solicit and listen to your input?

One person who understood the power of internal listening was the late Sam Walton, founder of Wal-Mart. Sam was a fanatic about visiting his stores, meeting with his associates, listening and learning and watching. One of the great Wal-Mart legacies began when he listened to one of his associates during a store visit back in 1980. As told in his autobiography, *Sam Walton: Made in America*, when Sam entered the Crowly, Louisiana, Wal-Mart, the first thing he saw was an older gentleman standing at the door, who, not recognizing Sam, quickly said, "Hi! How are ya? Glad you're here. If there's anything I can tell you about the store, just let me know." Once Sam learned that this man was serving the dual role of making people feel good about coming into the store and also making sure that no one left with unpaid-for merchandise, he immediately began spreading the concept of the "Wal-Mart Greeter" throughout his organization. Immediately spread? Well, it actually took Sam over a year and a half of relentless pushing to persuade all his stores to hire a greeter.[1] He often said that "99 percent of the best ideas we ever had came from our people."

Internal listening builds connections between the front line and the company. When customer-contact employees understand that their opinions matter just as much as those of the customer, their commitment rises. Whenever I think about the importance of internal listening, I am reminded of what Winston Churchill once said: "Courage is what it takes to stand up and speak; courage is also what it takes to sit down and listen."

Use Multiple Internal Communication Channels

Top managers often believe that as soon as their latest memo hits the mail room their work is done! That's all they have to do. Just send it out, with copies to everybody they can think of, and it's done. Better yet, group E-mail it and save postage! Many managers even have certificates from some business writing skills workshop to prove that they can write "powerful memos."

To connect with today's diverse employees, managers must intelligently employ any number of available and effective communication techniques. Small group and large group meetings, focus groups and work groups, videotapes and audiotapes, E-mail and "snail mail," television screens and computer screens, newsletters and form letters, bulletin boards and white boards are all effective tools in building connections. The January 1994 issue of *Meetings and Conventions* magazine reports that about 75 percent of Fortune 500 companies have in-house video-conferencing capabilities, which they use for everything from meetings and product introductions to company announcements. Even small businesses have such

[1]Sam Walton and John Huey, *Sam Walton—Made in America* (New York: Doubleday, 1992), pp. 229, 230.

capabilities through companies like Kinko's, which, in conjunction with Sprint, have installed videoconferencing equipment in more than 500 locations.[2]

The key to effectively using multiple internal communication channels is to keep messages simple. You do not need to create a complicated, highly sophisticated message suitable for an academy award nomination to connect with your communications. Sincere, straightforward, and to-the-point messages, regardless of the medium employed, are the most effective.

Encourage Two-Way Interaction

We have all heard about or experienced what management expert Ken Blanchard calls the Seagull Manager. A Seagull Manager, according to Blanchard, is a manager who seldom interacts with his people but occasionally swoops down into the workplace, dumps on everybody, and quickly flies away. There is no desire on the part of the Seagull Manager to interact with his employees or to hear what is really happening at the work site. So they swoop, dump, and leave. The obvious result is no connection between this manager and his employees.

Connection can occur only in an environment that promotes active two-way interaction among all employees. A great challenge facing most companies is transforming the traditional one-way, top-down communication into a flexible, two-way communication loop. Old habits die hard. For years we have recruited and trained gatekeepers, men and women with the express duty to keep other people away from us. To build connections and to gain the full commitment of employees, we must come out from behind our desks and embrace an "in-your-face" passion for employee interaction.

An in-your-face communication style is easier to adopt than you might think. Stop writing that memo and slide out from behind your desk. Walk down the hall and talk directly to the people you were going to write. Get out there and let

[2]*Meetings and Conventions,* January 1994, p. 17.

them see you. Give them a chance to get back in *your* face. Do not just ask for two-way interaction—demand it! Aggressively go after it. Make the connections so memorable that they will not be forgotten. If people are reluctant, that's OK, but keep it up. Get right back in their face again. Demonstrate your commitment to making the connection through two-way interaction.

Give Feedback in Real Time

Picture yourself on an operating table midway through your operation. The surgeon notices that an assistant is improperly performing his duty. Would you prefer that the surgeon make a mental note of this oversight and discuss it at the assistant's annual performance appraisal in seven months, or take immediate, real-time corrective action during the surgery?

Let's be a little less dramatic. I am a big fan of the University of Louisville's basketball team and of its Hall of Fame coach, Denny Crum. Just imagine him telling his players on the first day of fall practice, "It's going to be a long, tough year, but work hard and at the end of the year, we will let you know how well you have performed." Farfetched, I admit, but the very outrageousness of these two examples illustrates the essential need to give people immediate feedback.

When employees are not given feedback in real time, they tend to fill in the gaps in their knowledge with worst-case scenarios. For example, what goes through your mind when your daughter or son is an hour late coming home from a date? Do you imagine them safe and sound, laughing and enjoying good friends while the time innocently passes by (which is probably what is happening)? Or do you, like the vast majority of us, begin envisioning catastrophes? The car broke down and they are stranded; they have been arrested; or, worse yet, they have been in an accident and are being rushed to the emergency room of a hospital? We all tend to fill in what is unknown with these negative, worst-case scenarios.

Rumors are probably the most common result of withholding real-time feedback. Where do you think most rumors come from? Rumors begin when employees start filling in the gaps of an incomplete picture by supplying the missing information that should have been given them through immediate feedback. Real-time feedback minimizes the formation and impact of rumors. Immediate feedback helps rebuild the strained connections produced by rumors. By not delaying information, by quickly closing the communication loop through offering feedback in real time, managers can build strong connections with their employees that can withstand the storms of the future.

Best Practices

Here are twenty-two examples of how companies open communication with their employees.

1. "WHAT WOULD YOU DO?"

These four words are the foundation of one of the most powerful internal listening techniques available to managers. Many top executives, such as Ed Woolard, CEO of Du-Pont, are known for continually asking employees questions such as "What would you do if you were in my job?" Many fresh, innovative ideas, unencumbered by the traditional approaches or the psychological restraints imposed on people by their status in the hierarchy, can be uncovered simply by asking employees for their opinions.

2. "CRAYOLA PAYOLA."

Building on the proverb "A picture is worth a thousand words," the Philadelphia-based Rosenbluth Travel agency uses an old-fashioned communication system to connect with its employees. Occasionally employees receive a packet containing construction paper and a box of crayons and are asked to draw a picture of what the company means to them. Many positive, uplifting drawings have resulted. The real payoff of this rather unorthodox technique has been uncovering the negative feelings of employees, feelings that may have remained hidden. It has proved so effective that Rosenbluth now also sends paper and crayons to its clients for their impressions.

3. "LET'S RAP."

Hundreds of organizations now conduct "town meetings," gathering together large groups of employees for quarterly or monthly meetings. Motorola, the telecommunications giant, hosts quarterly face-to-face town meetings in which executives share the latest company news. They realize, however, that many employees may not speak up in such large group settings out of a sense of apprehension or embarrassment. So, after the town meeting, the executives hold what they call "rap sessions," break-out meetings with much smaller groups of employees to more effectively solicit two-way interaction.

4. "POST IT!"

Donnelly Corporation, the Michigan-based glass products manufacturer, creatively turns a very low-tech communication medium (posters) into a revolutionary technique. Throughout its plants are huge posters listing ten questions that all employees are encouraged to ask themselves, their colleagues, and their bosses. These questions include: "What made you mad today?" "What took too long?" "What cost too much?" "What is just plain silly?" and "What job involved too many actions?"

5. "ON-LINE TEAMS."

The phenomenal success of Boston Market (formerly Boston Chicken) is in part due to its intelligent use of on-line two-way communication. All managers at all levels collaborate on team projects via on-line computer links. Together, in real time, these project teams change menus, solve distribution problems, resolve customer complaints, and plan company expansions. Through a high-tech medium, Boston Market maintains a high-touch connection through real-time on-line teams.

6. "DODGI."

The Body Shop, the personal-care products retailer, is known for its progressive and often unconventional management practices. One tool it uses to open communication is known as the DODGI—the Department of Darned Good Ideas. Employees suggest ways to make things better, including suggestions as to how management can "ennoble your lives" and "make your spirits sing."

7. "ANONYMOUS RSVP."

A major reason why employees do not give senior management direct, specific feedback is the fear of retribution, of being singled out as a troublemaker or complainer. At the General Motors Saturn facility in Tennessee, they understand that some employees are reluctant to communicate to management what is really on their minds. Saturn therefore developed an electronic mail system that allows any worker to send *anonymous* messages to upper management and receive timely responses.

8. "YOU RANG?"

Creative ways of using the power of telecommunications are found in the most interesting places. An axle welder working in the massive John Deere & Company tractor manufacturing factory in Moline, Illinois, was getting annoyed. In order to obtain a needed spare part or to get an update on a particular item, he would have to walk all over the factory, wasting both his and his colleagues' time. So, what did he do? He did what any other progressive-thinking axle welder would do; he approached his boss about buying him a cellular phone! The boss quickly approved! The increased productivity has more than paid for the original investment. Cellular phones in a tractor factory? Ten years ago, who'da thunk it?

9. "POWER OF THE PAYCHECK."

New Hope Communications puts an interesting twist on communicating through its payroll system. Inside most pay envelopes, New Hope includes a sheet that asks for feedback in four key areas: the employees' happiness or unhappiness with their financial package; their feelings toward other employees; their feelings about the skills they are developing; and their overall feelings about their job. New Hope's innovative approach promotes real-time feedback to employees through tapping their opinions and needs.

10. "OPEN SPACE MEETINGS."

Cutting-edge companies are conducting what are called open space meetings, which are meetings having no agenda, no planned sessions, no scheduled speakers. The concept, created by Harrison Owen, an Episcopal priest and management consultant, has participants sit in a circle, and anyone who feels passionate about a topic (and is willing to lead a break-out session) can step into the center of the circle and announce his name and topic. The topic is written on a chart and posted on the wall. After all topics are listed, everyone participates in as many break-out groups as they desire to. Open space meetings allow employees from diverse areas an opportunity to create action plans to deal with their common concerns. Owens-Corning Fiberglass and Honeywell are just two of the dozens of companies currently using an open space meeting format to open communication and improve productivity.

11. "NICE TO KNOW YOU."

Ed Carter wanted to quickly build connections with his entire staff. Before he officially began as president of the Chicago office of Harza Engineering, he asked thirty top employees to complete a detailed survey that served as a basis for an in-depth, ninety-minute one-on-one discussion. He also scheduled weekly lunches, ten employees at a time, with all of the 140 other staff members, effectively building connections with every employee in less than twelve weeks.

12. "ONE THING BETTER."

A forward-thinking manager at the Mirage Hotel in Las Vegas initiated a simple two-way interaction activity between management and staff. Every month the manager asks her staff, "What one thing can I do better for you this month?" After listening and noting the employees' ideas, the manager then tells her staff, "Great, and here is one thing that all of you can do better for us this month." This technique builds connections between all employees while focusing on continuous improvement.

13. "FRIDAY FORUMS."

Every Friday morning at 9:00 A.M., more than 100 of the Symmetrix, Inc., management consultants meet for three hours of idea exchanges—that's *three hours!* Invitees include potential new hires, current clients, and prospective clients. There is only one rule if you attend: You must *actively* participate in the often animated and exciting debates.

14. "NOVICE CONSULTING."

Robert Kriegel, author of *If It Ain't Broke . . . BREAK IT!*, offers a great concept for opening communication through cross-departmental communication. Kriegel suggests that all employees be assigned the role of "novice consultant" and spend at least half a day shadowing a colleague in an area they know nothing about. Their task as novice consultants is to watch how their colleagues go about their work and to ask every conceivable question on what, why, and how things are done in that area. "Why do you do it that way?" and "How come you are doing that?" and "Have you ever thought of doing this?" are typical questions. This simple yet powerful tool is a cost-efficient way to open two-way communication while simultaneously injecting fun into the serious business of improving operations.[3]

[3]Robert Kriegel, *If It Ain't Broke . . . BREAK IT!* (New York: Warner Books, 1991), p. 137.

15. "6,000,000 REASONS."

One of the greatest examples of the return on investment for establishing internal listening as a priority comes from Ameritech, the Midwestern telecommunications group. The company's enterprising headquarters financial group hit the road to visit every major Ameritech office armed with a huge stack of company reports. In face-to-face meetings, the headquarters team would hold up each report and ask the field managers, "Do you really need this report?" Some reports were useful, others were consolidated, and many were simply eliminated. The team discovered that one well-intentioned and hardworking employee was spending five full days a month preparing and circulating a report that nobody read! Through this simple two-way interaction, Ameritech estimated that it eliminated the production and circulation of more than 6 million pages of reports.[4]

16. "MINUTE BY MINUTE."

During its application for (and eventual winning of) the Malcolm Baldrige Quality Award, the Cadillac Division of General Motors took an innovative, low-cost approach to timely employee communication through an already existing communication channel. Employees could hear updates on the status of their application via "The Baldrige Minute," a frequently updated message using the company's voice-mail system. It was an easy and effective way to open internal communication on an important company project.

17. "LINE 'EM UP."

Another Baldrige winner, the Ritz-Carlton Hotel Company, employs a powerful communication technique that significantly contributes to maintaining its world-class quality standards. Every day, every department of every Ritz-Carlton around the world conducts a fifteen-minute preshift

[4]*Fortune*, June 28, 1993, p. 130.

meeting called a "Line-Up" that focuses on what that department can do that day to improve service. Many departments also hold a fifteen-minute postshift "Line-Up" to discuss that day's progress and how to improve quality on tomorrow's shift. Internal two-way interaction with feedback in real time—that's a world-class practice all the way!

18. "QUARTER OF A MILLION STRONG."

Noel Goutard, CEO of the French auto parts manufacturer Valeo, aggressively combines internal listening and feedback to generate productivity improvement ideas. He personally holds all of his 25,000 + employees responsible for making at least ten suggestions for improvement each year, and every idea must receive a management response within ten days. Of course naysayers will think: "Yeah, but can you imagine the number of bad ideas?" Still, would you rather bet your career on a company that does not open communication for improvement ideas, or on one that generates a minimum of 250,000 employee improvement ideas every year?

19. "SAME DAY—YEAH OR NAY."

Many of us know the anxiety associated with waiting days or even weeks to hear the results of a job interview. The Disney Corporation takes feedback in real time very seriously, even for potential hires. After viewing a short, entertaining film outlining the basics of employment, applicants complete an application form and interview for a role (applicants are not "hired for a job" at Disney but rather are "cast for a role"). That very same day, all applicants are told whether they have been accepted or rejected. If rejected, they hear recommendations on how to improve and are invited to apply again in the future. Consider the message this sends all applicants, whether accepted or rejected, regarding the culture at Disney: Here, there will be fast, responsive, corrective feedback given within a positive, long-term framework. Care to apply tomorrow? You will get an answer—same day!

20. "SMILE FOR THE CAMERA."

Few executive teams have the courage displayed by the board of directors at Herman Miller in building connections with employees. All monthly officers' and directors' meetings at this Michigan-based office furniture designer and manufacturer are videotaped and distributed to its employees. Through opening the top-level meeting process for all to view, Herman Miller builds powerful connections with employees using a readily available communication technology.

21. "SPEAKER PHONE FRIDAYS."

A great way to give feedback in real time is employed by Ben Edwards, CEO of A. G. Edwards and Sons, the national stock brokerage firm. On the last Friday of every month, Edwards conducts a nationwide speaker-phone meeting. He begins the speaker-phone meetings with a brief state-of-the-company talk, then opens the phone lines for a real-time question and answer period.

22. "WORK IT OUT."

The ultimate in building connections, a technique that combines all four key strategies, is the famous "Work Out" sessions created by General Electric. Employee groups gather off-site for in-depth discussions and action plan development on key problems or productivity issues. Managers do not attend these discussions. Once the proposal is complete, managers join the meeting. Reports, overheads, graphs, charts, slides, and other visual aids add punch to the presentations. Then, in front of the entire group, the manager must make a decision—yes or no. (Rarely are decisions delayed for further review, and if they are, a decision must be reached within thirty days.) From internal listening as a priority to feedback in real time, all four strategies for building connections are found in this powerful, bottom-line strategy.

Action Ideas: How to Get On With It!

1. Pledge to yourself that for the next sixty days, whenever someone comes to you wanting a solution to a problem, you will ask, "What would you do if you were in my position?"

2. Use your E-mail system to send a "Focus for the Week" message. Challenge your team to list twelve ways in which the workplace was improved by the current focus.

3. Write your area's biggest problem on a piece of poster board. Send the poster board to another department and ask the people there to generate solutions.

4. End every meeting with one item that each team member pledges to improve before the next meeting. Designate a note taker to record everyone's improvement pledge. Review the pledges at the next meeting and reward successes.

5. Immediately begin a program creating cross-function internal consultants. Begin with yourself. Ask someone to volunteer to follow you around for one day and challenge everything you do with "whys" and "how comes" and "wouldn't it be better to" questions. Report the lessons learned back to the group. Then ask someone to follow your "consultant" for half a day within the next month, and continue the process.

6. Call a meeting with no agenda. Ask team members about their areas of greatest concern or areas they feel most strongly about. Allow the group to form small break-out groups to build action plans. Have the break-out groups share their action plans with the whole team. Then instruct the team to reach an immediate go or no-go decision.

Create Partnerships:
To Share and to Serve

"Ultimately, we're talking about redefining the relationship between boss and subordinate."

—Jack Welch, CEO, General Electric

A partner, according to *Webster's New World Dictionary, Second College Edition,* is "one of two or more persons engaged in the same business enterprise and sharing its profits and risks." *Webster* defines an employee as "a person hired by another to work for wages or salary." Consider the contrast between these definitions.

Partners are actively engaged in the business and have a direct stake in its success. Employees are simply hired for wages or salary. If given a choice between the two, which would you rather be—a partner or an employee? Under which definition would you put forth your best efforts? If you had a choice to surround yourself at work with either a group of partners or a group of employees, which would you choose? Only when we feel like fully participating partners do we voluntarily give our best to the organization. Today's best companies realize tremendous paybacks in productivity, profit, and commitment through creating strong partnerships with their work colleagues. Mediocre organizations continue to view their workers as "hired hands," as just another line item on the financial statements, no different from any other cost of doing business.

It's important to note what a partnership is not. A partnership is not a system of total equality. True partnerships do not mandate that everyone get exactly the same pay or even live within exactly the same bonus or incentive structure. No one expects the CEO to earn the same salary as a supervisor.

Additionally, a partnership does not mean a total democracy. Management must and should maintain its ultimate authority to overrule, readjust, or say no on key issues. The story of Kiwi Airlines is a good example. The original senior management pushed the noble concepts of democracy and equality so far that employees began ignoring executive directives. This resulted in significant disruptions, senior management turnover, and a continuing struggle for the airline to remain solvent and competitive.

The Partnership Facade

Here are a few familiar bromides to give you pause:

"We're one big happy family."

"Our employees are our greatest asset."

"We are all treated as equals around here."

"Teamwork is #1."

We have all heard these wonderful sentiments expressed at some point in our work lives. Well-meaning managers step to the forefront and bang the drums of "family" and blow the trumpets of "teamwork." Often, however, they march by themselves. Employees remain in the grandstands viewing these statements merely as a one-person parade. Bob Argabright, president of Chesapeake Packaging Company, says, "I've never seen a parade worth watching that only had a drum major." Why do such phrases ring so hollow within so many companies? Why do so many employees view these phrases with cynicism and dismay? How might employees respond to these phrases if given an opportunity?

Company: "We're one big happy family."
Employees: "So why not give *us* reserved parking, preferred stock purchases, weekend retreats, and glassed offices just like you?"

Company: "Our employees are our greatest asset."
Employees: "OK, but show us where (if at all) we are mentioned in the annual report, and what you are doing to increase the financial value of your 'greatest asset' through intensive training and development programs."

Company: "We are all treated as equals around here."
Employees: "Great, then we will place a time clock outside your office, join your bonus plan, and schedule you for the Christmas Eve shift so that we can be home with our families this year."

Company: "Teamwork is #1."
Employees: "Then why keep paying us for individual accomplishments, like individual sales or production quotas, rather than for achieving overall group goals?"

Creating Powerful Partnerships

An easy way to gauge the strength of your internal partnerships is to listen to the way your colleagues describe the company. People who feel a sense of partnership with the company continually use such words as *my* and *our* and *us* when speaking about their work. You hear them say things such as *"my* company," *"our* products," "it's all of *us* pulling together." By contrast, people who just feel like hired hands uses such words as *the* and *they* and *theirs*. You hear them say such things as *"the* company," "if *they* would only listen," "it's *their* problem."

Some companies change the words they use to describe each other in the hope of creating a stronger sense of internal partnership. Instead of calling each other "employees," they decide to refer to each other as "associates," "internal customers," "colleagues," "teammates," and, yes, even "partners." But just changing a few words without embracing the core strategies that actually create vibrant partnerships only creates a partnership facade.

Here are five strategies for creating powerful partnerships:

1. Squash status barriers.
2. Open the company books.
3. Pay for performance, not titles.
4. Share the bad times as well as the good times.
5. Serve the frontline partners first.

Squash Status Barriers

Status barriers are everywhere. From reserved parking spaces to executive-only bonus plans, status barriers eat at the heart of building resilient employee partnerships. I wish it were passé to discuss the negative impact status barriers have and how they erode the morale and commitment of employees. I also wish companies would recognize the often devastating psychological and emotional barriers that unnecessary status distinctions create between employees and the company. When employees live within a system of obvious "haves and have-nots," morale is usually low and performance is often marginal.

To create real partnerships, we must actively attack anything that artificially builds barriers between employees. As managers, we must ask ourselves some tough questions:

- How does reserved parking move the business forward?
- How does limiting performance incentives to the few inspire the commitment of the many?
- What is the impact of time clocks, docking pay, differential vacation or benefits plans, and probationary periods on our internal partnerships?
- How can we expect any employee to give his or her absolute world-class best if we promote and support a system that divides individuals into first-, second-, and third-class status?

The number of management layers between the front line and top management is a status barrier we often overlook. There are only two layers of management between the CEO and the newly hired eighteen-year-olds at many companies, including Quad/Graphics, the large Wisconsin-based magazine printer. There are only three layers of management between the CEO and the front line at ABB Asea Brown Boveri, the $29 billion European engineering firm with 215,000 employees across 140 countries. There are only five layers of management between Pope John Paul and all the parish priests in the 750-million-member worldwide Catholic Church! The greater the distance between the CEO and the front line, the greater is the perceived status barrier. One headquarters accounting group for a major company has an unimaginable eight layers of management between the clerks and the chief financial officer—and they are all located on the same floor of the same building! An unbelievable eight layers of "status" within one 4,000-square-foot office.

Perhaps the most obvious, artificial, and worthless status barrier in business today is created when managers force their staffs to refer to them as "Mr." or "Mrs./Ms." Many current managers were themselves forced to do this when they began their careers. They sometimes forget, though, how much they resented it and overlook the potential downside of forcing their own employees to conform. Regimented or involuntary salutations seldom lead to respect or help to create a sense of partnership or "corporate family." Can you imagine what your spouse or immediate family members would say if you told them to begin calling you "Mr." or "Mrs./Ms." to promote a stronger sense of family? To excite employees about our companies, we must assess and eliminate all status barriers that drive us apart.

Many status barriers are obvious, such as management layers and special bonuses, but the most devastating barriers are often subtle. Here is an example. A huge parking lot at a large company has a busy lane running next to the executive offices. On both sides of this wide, heavily traveled parking lane are two rows of parking spaces. One row faces the headquarters building, allowing the drivers to park their cars against the sidewalk curb just a few yards from the front door. The other row of parking spaces faces away from the building across the lane. One of these two rows of spaces is reserved for handicapped parking, the other for executive parking. Guess which row is for executive parking. Yeah, the row closest to the building is for the executives. Any handicapped visitors or employees must not only park farther from the building and fight lane traffic; they must also maneuver between the executives' cars to enter the building. (In all fairness, the building does have a wonderful ramp system for easy entry— once you get there.)

Open the Company Books

Jack Stack, president of Springfield ReManufacturing, is often heralded as the leader of the open book management craze sweeping the nation. Open book management, as the name implies, means opening the financial and operational statements to all employees. Stack believes that the best way to ensure the success of a company is through teaching everyone how to read the company's financial statements and learn how their function contributes to the company's profits. There is no better way, according to Stack, to help employees contribute to a profitable business than to teach them what a profitable business means to them and their specific areas.

Too many companies continue to operate under the out-dated philosophy of sharing the financial numbers with only a few select employees. Management groups continue to spend too much time deciding who should and who should not see the operational statements. Companies that fail to share key financials beyond just the basic sales and payroll numbers miss a golden opportunity to get everyone involved in growing a profitable business.

When an organization refuses to share the critical operational and financial numbers with all its employees, it implies that (1) it doesn't trust its employees; (2) it believes employees are not capable of understanding the numbers; and (3) it's not the employee's job to worry about the big picture. Wrong, wrong, wrong. First, if you do not trust your employees, why did you hire them? Second, frontline employees who can raise families on $400 a week can certainly comprehend an income statement or balance sheet. Third, a supervisor cannot effectively contribute to overall company profitability if she is limited to understanding just her individual department's numbers. Her maximum contribution to the company will occur only when she sees and learns how all aspects of the business contribute. Then she will be able to manage her area in the best interests of the company.

The more employees know about and understand their company's finances, the greater their feeling of partnership with the company is. Today's most progressive companies are forging open book systems involving all levels of employees. We should all strive to be like one open book company that, as it went public, had to cut back on the amount of information it typically shared with its employees.

Pay for Performance, Not Titles

Pay has traditionally been a function of the position you held in the company hierarchy. It is usually based on such things as responsibility, the number of people who report directly to you, and the amount of the budget you control. It represents an entitlement based on a title since the higher the position and the greater the span of control over people and budgets, the greater the pay is. Therefore, we focus more energy on how to get promoted than on how to add value to a service or product. We need to remember that a job title has never served a customer, repaired a machine, or improved a manufacturing process. Dedicated people serve, repair, and improve our company. In order to keep our best employees, we must refocus our pay efforts to reward actual performance rather than a mere job description.

Pay-for-performance programs are growing in popularity. They take many forms, including pay for knowledge, gain sharing programs, lump sum payments instead of raises, team productivity incentives, and employee stock option plans. The use of these systems will continue to expand, and for good reason. Employee commitment to company profitability and productivity increase when pay is directly tied to performance.

Progressive companies can create long-term partnerships with employees through pay-for-performance systems. It is common to find highly skilled, highly motivated, and wonderfully productive twenty-five- to thirty-year veterans at pace-setting companies like Lincoln Electric in Cleveland and Nucor Steel in Charlotte. As author and management consultant Michael LaBeouf says in his book *GMP—The Greatest Management Principle in the World*, "What gets rewarded gets done." Today's best organizations drive a spirit of partnership by rewarding performance, not titles.

Share the Bad Times as Well as the Good Times

Consider some recent events:

- A major U.S. airline conducts a four-day board meeting in Paris while simultaneously negotiating huge labor concessions from its unions.
- A Fortune 500 company cuts the salaries of 120 executive secretaries while granting millions of dollars in bonuses to the secretaries' bosses.

- A board of directors grants huge stock blocks and bonuses to executives for slashing thousands of jobs and closing down dozens of operations.

These occurrences are still all too common in American business today.

Michael Phillips poses a wonderful question in his essay "Labor as Trash" when he asks, "Is it ethical to fire twenty machinists and sheet metal workers who do good, consistent work, saving $700,000—instead of one vice-president with a $400,000 salary and $300,000 of expenses who made a major mistake in marketing?"[1] Rare are the announcements that senior managers are sharing the burden. Yet far too often are the announcements that management hoards profits in good times while greedily accepting huge bonuses during bad times. Such activities tear at the very soul of the vibrant partnerships necessary to win in today's marketplace. Even on Wall Street, the "share the wealth" mentality seems to have died.[2]

Living on the front line is a scary proposition. Headlines endlessly proclaim the elimination of jobs through layoffs, downsizings, closings, and restructurings. Most often the hardest hit is the front line. It is impossible to totally commit your heart, mind, and soul to an organization when you know that another group usually gets the lion's share of the "good" while your group usually takes the brunt of the "bad." Any successful business partnership is built upon a foundation of all parties equitably sharing both the good and the bad times.

Serve the Frontline Partners First

For close to twenty years, business experts have sung the praises of inverting the business pyramid. By placing managers at the bottom of the pyramid and the frontline staff on top, you demonstrate that a manager's key function is to support

---

[1]Michael Phillips, "Labor as Trash," in Michael Ray and Alan Rinzler, eds., *The New Paradigm in Business: Emerging Strategies for Leadership and Organizational Change* (New York: G. P. Putnam's Sons, 1993), p. 58.
[2]*Wall Street Journal*, February 9, 1994, p. C1.

the front line. For many, the idea of managers serving the front line first is still an extremely foreign concept. The "power of inversion" continues to remain the philosophy of the few. Many companies continue to enforce policies and procedures mandating that frontline employees serve management first.

A powerful example of how management continues to demand being served first is the sacred "operations manual." The overwhelming majority of operations manuals represent what the front line must do to make the job of managers easier. These manuals, filled with reports, forms, instructions, exceptions, returns, guidelines, lists, and justifications procedures, often choke the frontline staff's ability to serve the customer. One large company has a checklist for all the checklists its in-store managers must complete! In this kind of environment, who is serving whom?

The philosophy of serving managers first would appall the United States military. Companies love to use military metaphors when referring to their operations. "It's a war," "We need to rally the troops," "Let's dig in and win this battle," and "Don't give up the ship" are common corporate proclamations. Every organization that views itself as being in a "war" and enjoys using military metaphors to describe its competitive environment ought to remember the one absolute and unbreakable law that all U.S. military commanders must obey during the heat of battle: *Feed the troops first!* Yet many times we witness exactly the opposite in business. Management-driven activities (reports, forms, instructions, exceptions, returns, guidelines, lists, justifications) often force the troops (frontline staff) even in the heat of battle (serving the company) to serve management first. The internal partnerships can never occur within systems in which managers force the front line to serve them first.

A great example of why it is so important to create partnerships with your employees is something I learned in a seminar many years ago. The trainer offered this piece of advice: "If you take care of your people, they will take care of you. If you *don't* take care of your people . . . they will take care of you."

Best Practices

Here are twenty-five examples of how companies create partnerships with their employees.

1. "CORPORATE CASUAL."

Dressing down is the current rage all across America. Most progressive companies are adopting some combination of casual-dress days or weeks, while still others simply trust their employees to "do the right thing" in dressing for work. After Hurricane Andrew devastated Burger King's Miami headquarters in 1992, its then CEO, James Adamson, made some significant changes in operations, including the elimination of all executive suites and the addition of flextime to the benefits package. His reason for eliminating the headquarters dress code was the most touching. As Adamson noted, when the only clothes many of his employees owned the day after Andrew were "on their backs," he was reminded of how wonderfully people can perform in T-shirts and blue jeans.

2. "ADULTERY MANAGEMENT."

Years ago Chaparral Steel, the Midlothian, Texas, steel products manufacturer, decided that the best way to run its business was to build trust between employees. So, it simply began treating all employees as adults. For example, Chaparral never docks an employee's pay, and it doesn't believe in time clocks. Why? Because both are examples of *distrust* systems in which the real message is that a "company doesn't trust you at 8:00 in the morning, and they still don't trust you at 4:00 in the afternoon."[3]

3. "HIT ME WITH YOUR BEST SHOT."

The Los Angeles office of Chiat Day advertising takes an interesting and effective approach to minimizing both

[3]Robert Levering and Milton Moskowitz, *The 100 Best Companies to Work for in America* (New York: Bantam Doubleday Dell Publishing, 1993), p. 62.

status and stress. Punching bags hang in the break room with pictures of executives painted on them. Mad at the boss? Give 'im your best shot.

4. "THE HANDWRITING ON THE WALL."

One approach used by Manco, Inc. to open the company books is both interesting and effective. This Westlake, Ohio, building materials manufacturer places charts on its cafeteria walls that show key company numbers (sales, revenue growth, and productivity). Nothing so unusual there, except that the salesmen conduct weekly meetings to review their territories *in front of all employees* and seek everyone's ideas and suggestions for improving client sales and service.

5. "YOU CAN CALL ME RAY."

Whether the code is written or unwritten, a culture that mandates the use of formally addressing one another as Mr., Ms., or Dr. creates an often unnecessary barrier between employees. Recognizing this, First Federal Bank of California now makes it its formal, written policy to operate on a first-name basis. At East Jefferson General Hospital in Metarie, Louisiana, all titles, degrees, and departmental designations have been eliminated from name badges, making it easier for employees *and patients* to refer to everyone by his or her usual name.

6. "WE'RE ALL IN THE SAME BOAT."

At Springfield ReManufacturing, partnership pay follows a simple formula based on the philosophy that all employees should be part of the bonus program. Bonuses are calculated as a percentage of regular compensation. Whenever a bonus is paid, all employees get a check for an amount representing a preset percentage of their annual salaries. To encourage people to move ahead in the company, to take on more risks and responsibilities, the company makes most managers and professionals eligible for bonuses of up to 18 percent of their annual pay, and everyone else eligible for bonuses of up to 13 percent.

7. "THE ONE PERCENT SOLUTION."

The Xerox Corporation's Dallas-area operation is experimenting with a pay-for-performance plan that has one percent of every employee's pay linked directly to the area's ability to meet targets for customer and employee satisfaction, financial results, and quality. If the employees work together and meet the goals, they can double their money. If they fall short of the goals, they forfeit the money.

8. "PAY ME, PARTNER."

Plant employees at the San Francisco manufacturer North America Tool and Die occasionally have the chance to hand out paychecks to each other. Why do they do this? To remind everyone of the company's "I earn your pay, you earn my pay" philosophy. Beyond the obvious message of partnership, employees exchange much good-natured kidding as they tell each other how "I earned your pay—as usual" and "I'm sure getting tired of carrying you."[4]

9. "CAR WASH BLUES."

John Davis, a district manager with the Eckerd Corporation's Tennessee operations, knows the incredible power of building visible partnerships with the hundreds of associates working in his thirty-five drugstores. John's associates consistently win the company's prestigious and important store brand sales contest. What's the incentive for the store associates? John has a standing agreement: If his stores win the companywide contest, he will personally wash the car of every associate in the store with the best sales. He has gotten the "car wash blues" for three years running.

[4]Tom Melohn, *The New Partnership* (Essex Junction, Vt.: Oliver Wight Publications, 1994), pp. 85–86.

10. "BANK ON IT!"

Many companies, like Hi-Tech Hose, the Newburyport, Massachusetts, manufacturer, and the Charleston Area Medical Center, lump all vacation time, holidays, and sick days into one single account. Employees can then take time off whenever they need it and for whatever personal reasons. Hi-Tech Hose calls its plan the PTO—paid-time-off banks. Treating employees as responsible adults who are capable of managing their away-from-work time eliminates the stress generally associated with traditional systems. It also minimizes excuses for wanting or needing time off and eliminates the subjectivity usually associated with time-off requests.

11. "SHARE THE LOAD."

Rhino Foods, the Burlington, Vermont, specialty dessert maker, has a history of helping its employees during slow periods. To avert the sting of layoffs, Rhino arranges for workers to fill temporary work slots at other local companies, including Ben & Jerry's Homemade and Gardener Supply, a mail order firm. This "share the load" philosophy creates a more dedicated, loyal workforce.

12. "PROBATIONS BE GONE."

Many progressive companies have totally eliminated the practice of placing new hires on "probation" for some specified period. Organizations such as FedEx believe partnerships begin from the first day of work. Think about it this way: What is the first image that comes to mind when you hear the word *probation*? That's right, the prison system! What a joyous feeling it must be to know that you are going to be treated as a fully participating partner from day one. It's really quite simple. If you don't trust them, don't hire them!

13. "MANAGEMENT FIRST."

The senior managers at Delta Airlines understand their role as leaders in building partnerships during belt-tightening periods. When tough times require Delta to consider cutting the pay of employees, top managers first cut their own pay before taking action on other employees' pay.

14. "MANAGEMENT, TOO."

When Olin Corporation, the Stamford, Connecticut, chemicals company, restructured in 1994, it needed to get "lean and mean" at every level. But its approach to restructuring was unique in that Olin believed that "management has to set an example." How did the manager who led the restructuring set the example? By voluntarily eliminating his own position. Stupid, you say? Do you think the frontline employees would consider his move stupid? No, it's the ultimate in walking the talk of equally sharing the good and the bad times.

15. "PAY TO PLAY."

Outback Steakhouse takes an unprecedented approach to paying its restaurant managers as partners. The Tampa-based company asks its restaurant managers to sign a five-year contract and invest $25,000 of their own money in the restaurant; in return, Outback offers 10 percent of the unit's cash flow, paid monthly. If the unit is operated well, the managers can expect a six-figure income.

16. "NO SALARY."

A radical yet wonderfully successful approach to partnership pay is found at Lincoln Electric. Production employees at Lincoln receive no base salary, no hourly wage, no paid holidays, and no sick leave. Yet their productivity is often more than 200 percent higher than that of their competitors. The reason for this is Lincoln's ingenious piece rate and bonus system. Employees are paid for what they produce; the more pieces they produce meeting the quality standards, the more they get paid. The bonus is tied to overall company performance, which often doubles the employees' pay.

17. "ABOVE THE STANDARD."

Partnership pay is a longtime practice at the many Nucor Steel plants. Bonuses are paid when work exceeds predetermined standards. When employees produce 50 percent more than the standard, they receive a 50 percent bonus. If they produce 100 percent above the standard, they receive a 100 percent bonus. A motivating factor in Nucor's system is that the standard is not raised just because a lot of people are making a lot of bonus money.

18. "NONAUTOMATIC."

Prince Manufacturing of Holland, Michigan, assesses the performance of each new hire every three months for the first several years, then annually or *at the employee's request.* Pay rates can increase or they can decrease depending on the employee's attitude, quality of work, and how the employee follows basic work guidelines.

19. "DOUBLE YOUR PLEASURE."

Some of the most dynamic expressions of partnership occur in the wake of extraordinary employee efforts. One great example is when the management of the huge United Parcel Service's Louisville hub operation paid employees who were able to get to work during a blizzard twice their normal wage for that day. This was a simple yet powerful message, a share the good times thank-you for your efforts to build this business together.

20. "PARTNERSHIP PAIRS."

Penn Parking, the Baltimore parking garage management company, takes a very adult approach to scheduling its primarily teenage attendants. On every shift, two people are assigned each job. It is entirely up to the pair to determine who takes which days. Absenteeism and turnover are down and team spirit is up because employees are willing to cover for their partners when they know that one day they will ask their partners to cover for them.

21. "THE BIG SCREEN."

Jerry Ehrlich, CEO of Wabash National, uses a dynamic approach to sharing key operations information with his employees. Since Wabash is a tractor trailer manufacturer, what better way to drive home the importance of the numbers than to set up an overhead projector in the plant and project the financials on the side of one of the trailers!

22. "MOOV-IN DAY."

When freshman students arrive on the campus of the University of Texas in Austin, they are met by a strange sight. Dozens of senior university staff members and faculty stand ready, willing, and able to help them move into the residence halls. This highly visible and popular program reminds staff that they are there to serve the students. Since the University of Texas Mascot is a longhorn steer, the name of the program is "Moov-In Day."

23. "COFFEE CART BRIGADES."

During the busiest times of the year, executives at the Cigna Group Pension Division personally push coffee carts around the office while serving drinks and refreshments to their frontline partners. As they serve, the executives coach and encourage their colleagues as well as hear the real customer issues from those who know customer concerns the best.

24. "TAXI, TAXI."

When he became plant manager in the Mexico facility of Essilor of America, the international eye lens manufacturer, Dwayne Greer faced a severe third-shift turnover rate. After asking a few questions, Greer found the reason for the high turnover. The local public bus system did not run at night. It stopped its evening service to the plant several hours before the third shift began, and did not begin its morning service until several hours after the third shift ended. Employees working the third shift were thus forced to spend up to fifteen hours a day on-site. Recognizing a real win-win opportunity, Greer arranged for a local taxi company to pick up and drop off his third-shift employees at their homes. Within one year, this inexpensive program transformed a tremendous turnover problem into the enviable problem of having to manage a waiting list of employees and applicants motivated to join the third shift. What a wonderful example of a manager serving the front line first!

25. "1,000 x 2."

Creating partnerships is a way of life at Kwik Kopy. The headquarters staff call all 1,000+ franchise owners each month to make two requests: (1) Tell me one thing we can do for you, and (2) Please rate us on a scale of 1 to 10. The headquarters employee making the call is responsible for making sure "the one thing" gets done, and files a report on the request and the action taken. This maintains close contact with the field and allows headquarters to quickly spot trends that need attention.

Action Ideas: How to Get On With It!

1. Issue a "My name is" proclamation decreeing that the use of last names, titles, and formal salutations when addressing other employers is strictly forbidden. Anyone caught using them will be immediately fined 25 cents, to be donated to the coffee fund or a favorite charity.

2. Organize a facility's walk-through in which partners search for any subtle status barriers. Prioritize a list and begin eliminating or minimizing these barriers.

3. Begin a weekly thirty-minute "Number Crunchers" program to educate everyone on how to read and interpret the company's financial and operational reports. Invite other department or operations partners to discuss their areas, and how your department or operation affects them.

4. Hold quarterly "Fill in the Gaps" contests in which income statements with a few missing numbers must be cal-

culated by several teams. Allow the teams to use help sheets of financial ratios and calculators. When they are finished, determine which one or two line items need the most attention over the next quarter and assign a weekly "Recap Team" to monitor and report on progress.

5. Hold an off-site half-day brainstorming meeting with representatives from all company operations on the following topic: Titles and pay grades no longer exist at XYZ Company. How will we pay our best performers?

6. Create a roving "Snack Pack" of managers to roam the workplace distributing apples and cookies to employees while discussing current company issues with them. Require each "Snack Pack" member to return from this patrol with at least three items that need special attention.

7. Begin a monthly "Phone Tag Team" each of whose members calls another company operation (it could be next door or across the globe) and asks for two things they could do to help their colleagues. Create a list of the requests and review the trends to better anticipate internal partner needs.

8. Distribute to all frontline employees a quarterly survey that asks only one question: What can management do to better serve you? Organize a cross-functional team to create and circulate an action plan that addresses the top ideas.

Drive Learning: To Learn Is to Earn

"Perhaps the greatest competitive advantage to be enjoyed by an enterprise is the development of its human resources."

—*Journal of Industrial Training,* June/July, 1947

During a tour of his facilities, when I asked "What are the keys to success in your marketplace," a very successful and respected manager replied: "Hone your skills to perfection and learn something new every day." Nothing startling here, until you realize that the manager is Seferjin Aretis, head of the Youza Bread factory (formerly known as Moscow Bread Factory #19) located on a beautifully wooded hillside above the Youza River in Moscow. Should it be so startling that a Russian businessman sees learning as such a critical component of success? Certainly not. The point is that Aretis's bread and confectionery products plant was profitable and growing under the repressive Soviet system and today is still flourishing within the more open Russian economy.

Hone your skills to perfection and learn something new

every day. This should become the personal mission of every worker in America. All of us know that we must constantly improve our skills and increase our knowledge to keep up with the pace of business. Yet with the incredible pressure to just "keep our heads above water," self-development often goes on the back burner.

Fast Forward/Fall Behind

It seems that the faster the world moves today, the farther we tend to fall behind. There are good reasons for this:

- The amount of available information doubles every five years. There has been more information produced in the past thirty years than there was over the preceding 5,000 years.
- Within five years of graduation, half of what engineering students learn in college has become obsolete. Within ten years of graduation, less than one-fourth of their education is still applicable. According to the National Research Council of the Department of Labor, the so-called occupational half-life (the span of time it takes for one-half of a worker's skills to become obsolete) has dropped from between seven to fourteen years to only three to five years.
- In 1991, for the first time in history, companies invested more money in computers and communications equipment than in industrial, mining, farm, and construction equipment combined.

In 1985, who would have thought that over-the-road truck drivers would be using laptop computers and truck-mounted satellite dishes to give real-time updates on package delivery and location. Ten years ago, who would have thought that preschool-aged children would be talking to and sending computer-generated drawings via home computer modems to friends across the country and around the world. Ten years ago, who would have thought that a primary corporate agenda and a key strategic initiative would be a transformation into a "learning organization."

To successfully compete in today's fast-forward world, organizations must not allow their employees to fall behind in their knowledge or skills. The only long-term competitive advantage for any organization is the collective brain power of its people. With an entire staff of excited, brain-in-gear, cutting-edge thinkers, a company is always in a position to be an industry leader. Without an entire staff of excited, brain-in-gear, cutting-edge thinkers, a company is always playing catch-up to its competitors.

A fascinating irony in our fast-forward/fall-behind world is, as Michael Brown, CFO of Microsoft Corporation, states, "The only way to compete today is to make your intellectual capital obsolete before anyone else does." So it's not just a question of playing catch-up with our competitors' intellectual capital but rather a question of aggressively driving learning within our organizations so that we compete with ourselves to exponentially grow our internal intellectual capital.

Paying Lip Service to Learning

Employee training continues to receive more lip service than actual service. Organizations boast about how important training is and how employee learning is at the top of their agendas, but the reality is often the opposite. The American Society for Training and Development tells us that just one-half of one percent of all companies account for over 90 percent of the training conducted throughout the United States, and most of that training focuses on managers and executives, leaving the majority of workers on their own. A survey of 300 top executives by the international consulting company Towers and Perrin found that while 98 percent of the executives agreed that improving employee performance would significantly improve their company's productivity, and 73 percent claimed that employees were their company's greatest asset, investment in people actually ranked as their number 5 priority, behind customer satisfaction, financial performance, competitiveness, and product service quality.

Sadly, training budgets are often the first to get the axe during tough times, which is exactly the wrong thing to do. As management guru Tom Peters often proclaims, "When times are good, *double* your training budget. When times are bad, *quadruple* your training budget." So we often cut back on the one thing that can most help our employees during the toughest times, be it a massive organizational change, a restructuring or expansion, or even a simple shift in strategy within the marketplace. Driving learning throughout the organization is the best offense in a world of massive change and global competition.

Bury the Half-Truths

It's time to lay to rest the many half-truths associated with employee training. These conventional pieces of wisdom are simply no longer applicable. Managers and organizations that continue to cling to these half-truths fail to understand two key issues. First, they fail to realize that the only way to thrive in a knowledge-driven workplace is through knowledge-rich employees. It is ludicrous to expect a team of undertrained, knowledge-poor employees to compete successfully against a team of well-trained, knowledge-rich employees. Second, they fail to realize that knowledge-rich employees are the single greatest competitive asset an organization can have in our rapidly changing business world. Knowledge-rich employees are far more able and willing to help businesses maintain and increase their competitive edge and to support and lead the efforts necessary for corporate survival and growth. So let's bury forever the following five half-truths about training.

1. *"Train them and they will leave."* How wonderfully illogical! The converse of this proposition would read "So let's keep them employed with us and ignorant." Train your people well and, yes, a few will leave. But people—some of them

your best—leave anyway. A company that does not support its employees' professional development is far more likely to lose its best people. Great performers do not want to be dragged down by a company filled with mediocre or struggling performers. Further, by driving learning throughout your company, your recruiting becomes far easier because your reputation as an organization that develops its people is known. You will therefore attract the best people available, individuals who are self-motivated to improve. The most successful organizations take a "build it and they will come" approach rather than a "train them and they will leave" approach.

2. *"It costs too much"* or *"It's not in the budget."* Anything that improves the value of your business will cost something, whether it's a new piece of equipment, a new telephone system, or a facilities upgrade. If you believe that training costs too much, do three things. First, list the costs associated with one or two equipment investments that would most improve your business. Next, ask yourself how much the equipment would improve your business if your employees do not understand how to use it properly. Third, have your accountants calculate the cost of ignorance, that is, the estimated cost associated with a lawsuit from a product malfunction or the cost of injury from improperly using the equipment. The up-front cost of training is seldom anywhere near the potential downside of not training. Even with major equipment purchases, we budget dollars for maintenance and upgrades. Shouldn't we do the same for our single greatest asset—our employees?

An absolutely classic exchange occurred between an attendee at *INC* magazine's 1993 annual conference and a guest speaker, Jerry Ehrlich, CEO of Wabash National, who won the 1992 *INC* Entrepreneur of the Year Award:

> **Question:** "What would you say is the critical difference between an employee training program that works and one that doesn't?"
>
> **Answer:** "The sincerity of top management."

Question: "But how do people know you are sincere?"

Answer: "Because we spend ten times as much on employee education as we do on advertising."[1]

3. *"There's no return on training."* If learning creates little or no return on the investment dollar, why do so many parents want their kids to attend college? Parents understand the return on a son's or a daughter's college education. The lifelong value of education cannot and should not be measured on a short-term basis. It is amazing the number of parents who view a college education as a *long-term investment* (almost all of them), but who, as soon as they show up for work, view employee education as a *nonessential cost* (almost all of them). As Secretary of Labor Robert Reich says, "American companies have got to be urged to treat workers as assets to be developed rather than costs to be cut."

Well-designed, well-run training can create magnificent returns. Motorola calculates a 30 to 1 return on training; for every $1 it invests in training, the company gets back $30 in productivity gains within three years. After implementing a comprehensive companywide training agenda, its sales per employee doubled and profits increased almost 50 percent between 1988 and 1993. Motorola is just one of dozens of industry leaders like General Electric, McDonald's, The Home Depot, and Xerox that recognize the long-term returns on training investment.

4. *"We haven't got the time."* Remember the Law of 168: Everyone has exactly 168 hours per week, no more, no less. Your competitors operate under the same law. Whether you take the time for training or not, your competition probably does. For example, all management and union workers at the Saturn Corporation invest a minimum of 100 hours a year in training. Anderson Consulting, the $4 billion international consulting firm, has its tax advisers, auditors, and management consultants take 130 hours of training a year. Employees at Selectron, the high-tech component manufacturer, spend 110+ hours a year in training. These are but a few industry

leaders that maintain their leadership through lavishly investing time in employee training.

5. *"Training is not really the company's responsibility."* Yes, the ultimate responsibility for learning rests with the learner, just as the ultimate responsibility for career pathing rests more today with the employee than with the company. It is, however, a competitive necessity for a company to encourage and financially support employee learning. From basic reading and writing to advanced education, private business is now carrying the torch for training America's workforce. It's a question of choice. A company can choose to take responsibility for developing its brain power and remain competitive, or it can choose not to grow its brain power and risk extinction through the attrition of its best talent and the attempt to survive in a knowledge-based world with knowledgeless employees.

Imagine how ludicrous it would have been for General Colin Powell to have told his Pentagon staff two years before the highly successful Operation Desert Storm that freed Kuwait, "Hey, if we trained our people, they'll just leave, and anyway, it costs too much, we haven't got the time, and it's really not our responsibility." Would you want to be a soldier in that system? Would you want to be an investor in that system?

To inspire the long-term commitment of your employees (and to better ensure the long-term viability of your organization), you must drive learning throughout your operation by following three key strategies:

1. Guarantee employability, not employment.
2. Promote visible, action-filled learning.
3. Encourage continuous, lifelong learning.

Guarantee Employability, Not Employment

The list reads like a who's who of businesses. AT&T Communications Systems. Allied Signal. General Electric. Allstate Insurance. Raychem. Corning. What do these great companies have in common? Certainly not industries, markets, or customer bases. They do, however, share a vital approach to gaining the confidence and commitment of their employees. Instead of a guarantee of *employment,* these companies guarantee something far more vital to an employee's future— *employability!*

An employment guarantee suggests that a company will always have a job available for an employee. We all recognize that this is no longer a reasonable guarantee. The incredible pace of business today prohibits any group from offering anyone a rock-solid guarantee of a job for life.

An employability guarantee is quite different. When a company offers a guarantee of employability, it promises to provide employees with every possible opportunity for professional improvement, so if their jobs are ever eliminated, they will be so employable that they can easily find work in another department or another company. Larry Bossidy, CEO of Allied Signal, says, "We can't guarantee permanent jobs, but while you work here you will have the opportunity to develop talents that will serve you well with us or [as you] move on." Andria Miles, manager of employee selection and staffing at Corning, believes "It has become more and more important to let people know that you are offering them a chance to develop skills that are marketable anywhere."

Most companies still take a one-volume approach to employee learning. Even if they have an entire A to Z library of learning opportunities, they allow most employees to view only the one volume most closely associated with their jobs and prevent them from participating in other programs. It's as if a child who had completed reading the *A* volume of an encyclopedia set and wanted to go on to *B* were told by his father: "No, son, you are not allowed to read the other volumes. Let's see if we can find you an advanced *A* volume."

Employability is a vital part of gaining the long-term commitment of employees. People are far more likely to invest their complete energies in a company when it helps them to grow, to experience new and different aspects of the business, and encourages their full development beyond the original job description. Focusing efforts on long-term employability is a key strategy in creating an enthusiastic (and talent-rich) employee base.

Promote Visible, Action-Filled Learning

Employees know when a company is committed to the development of its people. The evidence is all around them— training class schedules, external learning options, company-sponsored lunchtime learning sessions, on-the-job training, guest speakers at company meetings, tuition grants and reimbursements, company libraries with books and tapes available for checkout, cross-training and career development programs. Everywhere they turn they see the signs of a company that is dedicated to their development.

Perhaps the most powerful visual cue is getting everyone in the organization involved in learning. Can a frontline cash register operator teach a CEO anything? You bet she can. Can a CEO teach a frontline cash register clerk a few things? Absolutely. Everybody, then, can be both a learner and a teacher. The best organizations drive learning up, down, and laterally into every nook and cranny of the company. They maintain that no one is too busy, no job title too exalted, and no group either too high or too low to be excluded from the process of learning.

Peter Senge, author of *The Fifth Discipline: The Practice of the Learning Organization*, defines learning as putting knowledge into action. Adults learn best when they are actively involved in the learning process, not when they are merely passive recipients. Action-filled learning is a great way to increase retention and to visibly demonstrate a commitment to employee development.

Encourage Continuous, Lifelong Learning

Imagine this scenario. Your dentist, physician, and pharmacist all graduated with honors from their medical schools. Your dentist graduated in 1962, but hasn't been to a professional conference in decades. Your family physician graduated in 1973, but years ago stopped subscribing to the many medical journals he once loved to read. Your pharmacist graduated in 1988, but studies only enough to maintain her certification. How would you feel about sending your family to these professionals? Would you feel safe and secure about their prognoses? Would you hope that the medical professionals your family currently consults are dedicated to a lifetime of continuous learning?

The concept of lifelong learning is not new. Honeywell began serious initiatives in lifelong learning in the mid-1980s. General Motors' NUMMI (New United Motor Manufacturing, Inc.) facility transformed its most unproductive auto factory into its best through a focus on lifetime learning, with the additional benefit of seeing absenteeism drop from 24 percent to 3 percent and employee satisfaction rise to 90 percent. At the Tokyo restaurant Chinsan-so, there is a progression of curriculum beginning with eighteen-year-olds, another for twenty-five-year-olds, and another for thirty-five-year-olds, and still another for forty-five-year-olds. That's a twenty-seven-year curriculum for employees in a restaurant! Amazingly, most of the employees end up progressing through each stage![2]

We can no longer expect employees routinely to give their best efforts throughout their work lives to organizations that refuse to help them grow throughout their lifetimes. Lifelong learning must now be considered a standard job benefit and a core ingredient in your operating plan. In their book *The Monster Under the Bed*, Stan Davis and Jim Botkin state that "public school systems do not have the right format for providing the kind of lifelong education that will best serve the future needs of our economy and our society."[3] A critically important element in shaping the future success of any business is the energy and resources it focuses on the lifelong learning of its employees. As a former boss and a respected human resources senior manager is fond of saying, "No

[2]Center for Creative Leadership, *Issues and Observations*, Vol. 13, No. 4 (1993): 1–2.
[3]Stan Davis and Jim Botkin, *The Monster Under the Bed* (New York: Simon and Schuster, 1994), p. 19.

organizational improvement is possible with unimproved people."

Best Practices

Here are thirty-two examples of how companies drive learning throughout their organizations:

1. "LOYALTY, SCHMOYALTY."

Sandoz Pharmaceuticals Corporation tells employees it is no longer disloyal for them to consider career paths that lead outside the company. Sandoz believes that offering employees ways to enhance their future employability both alleviates the anxiety connected with losing a job and demonstrates that the company truly cares about them as people.

2. "NOT READY FOR PRIME TIME."

The idea of promoting someone into a position for which he or she is not fully trained seems ludicrous to most companies, but most companies are not as progressive in their employee development as J. P. Morgan. This New York Investment company routinely promotes employees into positions that stretch their abilities and force them to learn and grow. Instead of filling positions with overqualified candidates who may quickly lose interest and enthusiasm, Morgan's "Not Ready for Prime Time" philosophy keeps employees interested and excited.

3. "ELECTRONIC RÉSUMÉS."

Because computer proficiency is an absolute must in running a successful international consulting company, McBer and Company accepts no paper résumés. Applicants must apply through sending a fax or shipping their credentials to McBer via a computer disk. What a great way to drive learning, even for those applicants you choose not to hire.

4. "Game of the Week."

McBer and Company also encourages employees who may be computer-shy or beginners on the keyboard to play the computer "Game of the Week." Each week a new computer game is chosen to help make learning fun and the computer less threatening.

5. "Hello, Trolley."

It is never too soon to begin lifelong learning or to prepare prospective employees for careers. The Mansfield and Green Division of AMETEK, the global technology manufacturer, in conjunction with the local school system, renovated an old school bus to create a mobile learning center called the BAMA Trolley. Area seventh graders can climb aboard and conduct twelve different hands-on experiments using actual calibrators and gauges manufactured at AMETEK. This program promotes careers in manufacturing and is a magnificent example of visible, action-filled learning.

6. "70-30 Learning."

Springfield ReManufacturing, the progressive Missouri-based truck engine and parts repair company and one of the first to adopt open book management, drives learning from the first day of employment. All new hires are told that "70 percent of your job is to do your part in rebuilding truck engines, 30 percent of your job is to learn how to make a profit!" Yes, it is a very profitable company, and the learning associated with making a profit starts from day 1. As CEO Jack Stack says, "When you appeal to the highest level of thinking, you get the highest level of performance."

7. "Required Reading."

Within the first ninety days of their employment at ipd Co., the auto parts manufacturer, President Richard Gordon orders all new employees to read the book *The Power of Ethical Management.* He has also created a "Learn and Earn

Program" in which employees are paid for preparing reports on what they have learned from reading books, listening to tapes, or attending seminars. The addition of a small
library adjacent to the lunchroom also drives learning at
ipd.

8. "LEARN ALL YOU CAN."

Johnsonville Foods, the Wisconsin sausage maker, is one
of many great companies that encourage employees to attend any company-sponsored training class regardless of its
direct applicability to their current jobs. Johnsonville believes that all learning is valuable, whether it can be used
at work or at home, now or in the future. It also encourages
every employee to spend one day a year with another employee to learn more about the company.

9. "T-SHIRT LEARNING."

During a quarterly meeting at one of the Iams Company
plants, the company president challenged all employees to
remember four key business goals. He announced that
there would be a "quiz" on the four areas at the next meeting. To inject some fun into the assignment and to drive
learning, the plant distributed to all 150 of its employees T-
shirts with the four goals printed on the front. Every day,
somebody in the plant would be wearing his T-shirt, re-
minding everyone of the goals. At the next quarterly meeting, the whole plant passed the quiz.

10. "TRADING PLACES."

One powerful way to encourage two-way learning is
through living the adage of "walk a mile in my shoes." At
Beth Israel Hospital in Boston, doctors occasionally dress
as maintenance staff and roam the hospital halls. Why? To
learn how it feels to be treated as "support staff" and to
find ways of improving the hospital environment. (Please
note that we have been assured that the maintenance staff
does not roam around in surgeon's garb to test operating
room procedures.)

11. "50% +."

One company that understands the power of two-way learning is Nordstrom. Corporate buyers spend 50 percent of their time in the stores talking to customers and sales staff, meeting with vendors, and learning in the trenches. When times are bad, the buyers spend even more time in the stores!

12. "90-Day Training Cycle."

Learning should start at the top, just as it does at PepsiCo. when CEO Craig Weatherup gathers together his top senior managers to decide which is the one company area in most urgent need of immediate improvement, he gives himself and his staff ninety days to do two things: (1) learn all they can about how to improve that area, and (2) train their direct reports in that area. The newly trained middle managers are then, in turn, given ninety days to learn all they can and to train their direct reports, and so it goes throughout their worldwide operations. When the first ninety-day cycle is complete and all next-level managers have been trained, Weatherup again gathers his top senior managers to decide on the *next* area in need of immediate improvement, and the training cycle continues.

13. "Teacher, Teacher!"

After working their standard forty-hour shift, employees at the magazine printer Quad/Graphics are offered a completely voluntary day of training. The classes are frequently full. Want to teach a class? Any employee who finds just three others interested in a topic can teach a class on it— but only after attending a class that teaches people how to teach adults. The topics allowed—anything the employees want, whether it pertains to job knowledge or life knowledge.

14. "Read All About It."

Learning and continuous improvement have become an unwritten way of life at companies like the public relations firm Cunningham Communications. All employees—that means everyone, including secretaries and other support staff—are encouraged to read at least one hour a day, be it trade journals, newspapers, business magazines, or anything else connected with public relations. Imagine the organizational learning that takes place in an environment that focuses daily attention on reading, absorbing, and passing along industry-specific knowledge.

15. "YOUTH MANAGEMENT DAY."

A longtime tradition at Winn Dixie supermarkets is "Youth Management Day," on which more than 800 part-time employees between the ages of fifteen and twenty take over store management for the day. It encourages young employees to consider a career with the company and allows managers to assess managerial potential. To better prepare them for the big day, Winn Dixie sends each youth manager through one full week of training.

16. "BOOK LEARNING."

A business that many throughout the western United States would argue is the best bookstore in the country, Denver's Tattered Cover is a staunch believer in learning. All new hires receive two weeks of sales training. The first day is taught by Joyce Meskis, the owner.

17. "TEN-MINUTE HUDDLES."

To drive real-time learning, the Eckerd Corporation's Dallas region drugstore managers conduct what they call "Ten-Minute Huddles." These ten-minute store pre-opening meetings focus on key operations areas and cover everything from selling techniques and merchandise displays to customer service tips and generating suggestions for store improvement. The real-time flexibility of the "Ten-Minute Huddles" has improved service delivery and employee commitment throughout the region.

18. "I Know Nothing."

To challenge thinking, Honda Motors deliberately places individuals who know nothing about technology on the company's design teams. Great innovations arise from the spirited discussions that flow from the "I know nothing" questions and probings.

19. "ChooChooU."

Dean Junior College in Franklin, Massachusetts, teaches college classes to students while they ride the morning commuter trains to Boston! Students at "ChooChooU" range in age from their early twenties to their seventies. According to the teachers, the challenges in teaching these classes include learning how to remain standing on a moving train, keeping the easel from falling, and speaking above the noise.

20. "Kaizen Carts."

Cummins Engines has a simple yet powerful way to drive learning throughout its truck engine factories. After employees attend an intensive quality training program, they can then use the "kaizen carts" spread throughout the facility. These portable metal carts are loaded with pens, pencils, stopwatches, easels and scratch paper, books and reference materials, tape, erasers, calculators, and all kinds of materials. They can easily be rolled into any production area and used to help teams address quality, process, or production problems on the spot. The kaizen carts are a sign that a department is improving, which encourages all other departments to roll a cart into their areas to improve their operations.

21. "Call Back."

Restek, the lab equipment manufacturer in Bellefont, Pennsylvania, drives learning through a customer service program that is tied to employee bonuses. Employees can volunteer to call back customers to learn what the customer thinks of their products and the company. An added benefit of this program is the learning that occurs when employees return customer calls with answers to questions they have researched.

22. "CHOW DOWN."

Once a month, any employee of Allen Susser's Chef Allen's restaurant can go out to dinner at another restaurant with a spouse or a friend and Susser will kick in up to $50. The only condition is that the employee must write a one-page report on the experience and give an oral report before the entire staff. By supporting his employees in observing other restaurant operations, Susser drives learning on what customers see as quality food service.

23. "IN-TOUCH TRAINING."

The Home Shopping Network executive staff can occasionally be found answering incoming customer calls at their various studio sets. What they call their "In-Touch Training" does exactly that—keeps them in touch with both customers and frontline employees.

24. "SEVEN SEMINARS."

Computer chip maker Intel Corp. requires all its employees to attend seven seminars in their first year of employment. Led by senior managers, the seminars focus on the corporation's culture, values, and business ventures. Titles range from "What Makes Intel, Intel," "The Intel Culture Class," and "All About Intel, Our Business and the Customer."

25. "20% A YEAR."

Few companies take so progressive an approach to training and retraining employees as Allstate Insurance does. To help employees keep their skills updated. Allstate's goal is to completely retrain everybody in the company every four to five years. So every year, all employees focus on improving and upgrading their skills in at least 20 percent of what they do, creating an environment of constant, lifelong learning.

26. "TIPS."

Learning does not have to be packaged in long, multiple-day sessions. Every two weeks, Conners Communications, a New York public relations firm, offers a fifteen- to thirty-minute program on topics of employee need. The series is nicknamed TIPS, for "Tips for Improving Performance Sessions."

27. "EASY ACCESS."

The Oklahoma City office of All American Bottling found a low-threat way to encourage its computer-leery accounting staff to overcome its apprehension. In the middle of their general work area, the company set up a personal computer loaded with every imaginable kind of software. Staff members were asked to just play with it as they wished. Before long, clerks with no previous computer knowledge were operating spreadsheets, tracking customers, creating newsletters, and having friendly fights as to whose turn it was on the computer.

28. "GATE-WAY TO LEARNING."

Essilor of America, the prescription eyewear manufacturer, rewards its learners in an innovative way. It offers a GED-equivalency program called GATE (Getting Ahead Through Education) in which employees are given one hour of compensation time for every ten hours of class time. Many use the accumulated time for such activities as Christmas and holiday shopping, going fishing, or enjoying a three-day weekend.

29. "LIVE THE SPIRIT."

To encourage lifelong learning, Philadelphia-based Rosenbluth Travel sponsors monthly seminar programs for its employees that benefit both personal and professional life.

Topics range from handling difficult situations, goal setting, and dealing with change to food, fitness, and recycling. There is a new topic every month in what Rosenbluth calls its "Live the Spirit" programs, so all employees across the country are learning at the same time.

30. "FOUR-MONTH FOCUS."

The Industrial Controls Group of Allen-Bradley, the Milwaukee auto parts manufacturer, created a powerful program to drive employee learning. The employees choose three topics a year to explore in depth. Each topic then becomes the focus of four months of intensive training and learning. Everything from in-depth discussions to information posted on bulletin boards and articles in newsletters drives learning on each topic while it is the focus of attention.

31. "CUSTODIAL OLYMPICS."

Teams of custodians at Texas A&M University hold an annual event designed to test and improve their professional skills on everything from dust mops to floor waxers. Just like the real Olympics, these "Custodial Olympics" have preliminary meets in such key events as the "Peanut Push" and the "Obstacle Course," with finalists competing for awards and bragging rights. Staff practice for weeks before the Olympics to improve their skills with all the equipment. The learning permeates the whole campus because all practice sessions, preliminary meets, and the Olympics themselves are performed out in the open—in front of students! The students gain a newfound respect for the professional skills of the custodians, and the custodians thrive on the friendly competition. Recently, Texas A&M challenged some other Texas campus custodial staffs for state bragging rights.

32. "BOZO BOXES."

Sequent Computer Systems of Beaverton, Oregon, takes a fun approach to driving learning regarding the importance of treating customers and suppliers with courtesy. Everywhere you look in its facilities you see what are called "Bozo Boxes." Anyone caught badmouthing, criticizing, or complaining about a customer or supplier must put a quarter in the nearest Bozo Box. The proceeds go to charity, and the process keeps everyone humble and focused on having a positive outlook toward all business partners.

Action Ideas: How to Get On With It!

1. Adopt another department in your organization. Teach members about your function and how it relates to them, the overall company goals, and the customers.

2. Invite colleagues from other departments to speak at your staff meetings about their areas.

3. Challenge yourself and your team to learn five new business concepts a month. Include anything from financial ratios and marketing or production concepts to legal obligations.

4. Create an "I bet you didn't know" club. Allow each member to share one company fact or piece of company trivia with the group. Discuss how each fact affects operations.

5. Total the hours you spent last month with the frontline employees. Take out your calendar for this month and double it!

6. Schedule five- to ten-minute meetings at the beginning of each day to let staff members share their key goals for the day. End the day with a five-minute recap of accomplishments and new concepts learned.

7. Sign up your department/area with an on-line computer service that accesses business headlines, news, and industry publications. Assign employees to a rotating schedule of scanning articles, reports, and stories. Sponsor biweekly meetings to review the latest news and industry happenings.

8. Sponsor a "No Paper Week" in which no one in your department/area is allowed to generate any paper for another

department member. Fine any paper generator 25¢ toward a department cookies and soda celebration at the end of the week.

9. Conduct a "This Is What I Learned This Month" departmental lunch. Require everyone to share at least two things they learned this month about company operations, key customers, industry trends, service or product improvement, or nonjob-related learning.

10. Circulate an "I really wish I knew . . ." list (perhaps via E-mail) requesting employees to list those areas they feel they need to improve, learn more about, or just keep up with. Use the list to begin cross-training, to encourage individual and group learning, and to develop individual learning programs.

11. Hold a monthly "At the Movies" afternoon break, complete with popcorn and snacks. Show a training or industry-related video (easy to find, cheap to rent). Ask for a "thumbs up" or "thumbs down" vote on the movie's relevance to your industry, applicability of ideas, even its Oscar potential! Discuss how to implement the ideas generated by both the movie and group discussion in order to improve your organization.

Emancipate Action: Free at Last, Free at Last!

"The idea of liberation for our workforce is not enlightenment—it's a competitive necessity."

—Jack Welch, CEO, General Electric

Abraham Lincoln considered it the greatest thing he ever did. He crafted a document that would capture the human spirit and rally support for his commitment to freeing all slaves within the territories at war with the Union during the Civil War. Lincoln chose to call his document the "Emancipation Proclamation." It read: "All persons held as slaves are and henceforth shall be free." Lincoln's documents created freedom from restraint while mandating an unconditional release from bondage, servitude, and serfdom.

Lincoln did not call his document the "Empowerment Program." *To empower* means simply "to permit." Permission, with its cold, confining, emotionless flavor, is a far cry from the concept of liberation. If Lincoln had wanted to create an

"Empowerment Program," his document might have read: "All persons held as slaves are and henceforth shall be *permitted to make certain personal and professional decisions that fall within well-defined policies, procedures, and guidelines.*" Can you imagine Lincoln running around Washington excitedly displaying his "Empowerment Program"? Can you imagine the reaction to such a program, especially from those he wished to "empower"?

Emancipation Imagination

Imagine a caged eagle. Imagine an eagle confined in a box surrounded by metal bars and doors. Regardless of someone's sincerity in yelling "you're empowered, you're empowered," a caged eagle can never soar. A caged eagle can never control its surroundings or reach the potential that lies within.

How many times do we intentionally or unintentionally cage our company's eagles? How many times do we say "you're empowered, you're empowered" only to slam shut the cage door with "be sure to follow all the checklists [*slam*] and don't spend over $15 without prior approval [*slam*] and don't change the work schedule [*slam*] and be sure to get my OK before you do that [*slam*] and be sure to fill out the forms or the audit department will make a house call [*slam*] and . . ." The sound of slamming cage doors continues to echo all across America.

Regardless of its talents or potential, a caged eagle can at best only conform to the dimensions of its cage. But when it is released, no one need shout encouragement to it to soar, no one need hang motivational slogans on its nest exhorting excellence. When unleashed from the shackles of bureaucracy, when freed from the confines of an operational prison, eagles study their surroundings, spread their wings, and fly! No "empowerment program" ever written comes close to true liberation.

It is time for American business to rethink its motivation process. If a hefty portion of it does not include true emancipation, a fundamental unshackling from bureaucracy, we are simply shouting "rah-rah" to a bunch of caged eagles.

Emancipation Application

A popular misconception is that any movement toward a truly emancipated workplace creates anarchy. Emancipation does not create anarchy. Employee actions must be coordinated. The key is to determine *how often* and *how much* employee action must be regulated or okayed from above. My definition of emancipation is simply giving people the *freedom to succeed,* as opposed to empowerment, which is *permission to follow policy.* As one boss told me years ago when I asked him what I should do with the company's eight-inch-thick notebook containing policies and procedures, "They make great doorstops." And he was right; they did.

Emancipation is giving people the protection they need to excel, the power to control their own destinies, and then getting out of the way! As management guru Peter Drucker says, "Management's job is to find out what it's doing that keeps people from doing a good job, and stop doing it." Most often, this means simply getting out of the way of the people who do the real work. An intensive multiyear study conducted during the early 1990s by Sibson & Co., a San Francisco–based consulting firm, supports this view. The results of its study, based on focus groups of more than 50,000 employees around the world, found that employees basically want to do their jobs, do them well, and contribute to a successful company, and want management to get out of their way and let them do it.[1]

A great example of emancipation in action occurred when a newly hired manager asked the chairman of his industry-leading, international high-tech company what he, the manager, should do in his job. At most companies, the answer would have been to work hard, follow guidelines, and stay within budget. But this chairman simply replied, "Do some-

[1]*St. Petersburg Times,* January 17, 1993.

thing great!" When was the last time your boss asked you to do something great? Has anyone ever asked you to do something great?

General George S. Patton is considered one of the greatest battlefield generals of the twentieth century. His campaigns were brilliant—well coordinated, daring, and successful. Patton's success in large part grew out of his belief that "a good plan violently executed now is better than a perfect plan next week" and "if everyone is thinking alike, then someone isn't thinking." To violently execute a good plan now and encourage diverse thinking are great examples of the potential power of emancipation.

There are four key strategies involved in emancipating the action of employees.

1. Allow freedom to fail and try again.
2. Create freedom from bureaucracy.
3. Encourage challenges to the status quo.
4. Give everyone input into firing the right customers.

Allow Freedom to Fail and Try Again

As a kid, I grew up playing a lot of baseball. I dreamed about being able to hit the ball like Hank Aaron, Willie Mays, and Mickey Mantle, and of pitching like Sandy Koufax and Bob Gibson. They were my heroes then and they continue to be my heroes today. Did you know that there were more than 8,000 times during his career when Aaron failed to get a hit? Mays failed to get a hit almost seven out of every ten times he batted. Mantle struck out more than 1,700 times. Koufax did not have a winning season until his seventh year in the big leagues. Gibson lost 40 percent of all the games he ever pitched. Yet these men are all Hall of Famers, considered among the greatest ever to have played the game. How would your organization react to such failure rates? If these men were employees in your company, would they be inducted into the company's "Hall of Fame" or its "Hall of Shame"?

Think about how most organizations respond to failure. Most companies do everything they can to prevent failures, to keep mistakes from happening. They overregulate and over-stipulate in an attempt to control every possible contingency in which employees might make mistakes. And if a mistake happens, it often calls forth a "hide it, cover it up, don't bring attention to it because we might get in trouble" mentality. Companies end up paralyzing themselves, squelching any attempt at the new or different because of a general fear of failure. But, as Fred Smith, founder of Federal Express, says, "Fear of failure must never be a reason not to try something different."

Perhaps our greatest challenge is to create a culture that allows freedom to fail and try again while tenaciously pushing everyone toward taking their best shots. Just consider all the innovations that are never tested, all the productivity-improving ideas that are never tried, all the brilliant customer service strategies that are never enacted because of environments that condemn failure. The "I don't care what you do, just *don't make a mistake!*" workplaces never create Hall of Fame careers. As the greatest scorer in the history of professional hockey, Wayne Gretsky, says, "You miss 100 percent of the shots you never take."

So should we advocate freedom to make any and all mistakes? No. We must draw the line when an employee is about to make a mistake that threatens the organization's survival or, even more important, may cause physical harm or death to a colleague or customer. Should a grocery store manager knowingly allow a butcher to display outdated meat? Should an instructor allow a student to jump from an airplane with an improperly packed parachute simply so that that student will have an opportunity to "learn" from her mistakes? That clearly would be ridiculous. Anything short of actions that might cause irreparable organizational or personal harm, however, should be considered for positive experimentation.

Years ago a man visited a facility of a successful high-tech company with a long history of allowing employees the freedom to fail and try again. While chatting with the plant manager, the visitor heard a thunderous boom. Jumping out of his chair, he shouted, "What was that?" The plant manager calmly said that it was the plant's cannon being fired. The quick-thinking guest asked, "Do you always shoot off a cannon at 3:41 P.M. on Thursday afternoons?" The plant manager said "No. We shoot the cannon to let everyone know that another one of our experiments just blew up, that we failed; but to us, hearing that cannon means [*holding his thumb and first finger an inch apart*] we're *that much closer to success.*" Pure freedom to fail and try again.

When employees are given opportunities to experiment, to try new things, to use their brains, their commitment soars. And even if some experiments or pilot tests or good plans violently executed blow up, so what? Your company will still be light-years ahead of your competitors, because most of them continue to live within systems that would rather play it safe and remain mediocre than risk even temporary failure. On the last page of his book *Liberation Management,* management authority Tom Peters summarizes this important strategy when he states that "all too often we forget that freedom to fail and try again is the essence of liberation, in America and elsewhere."

Create Freedom From Bureaucracy

While visiting my sister in Dallas, I drove to a nearby branch of a nationally known supermarket chain, found my three items, and headed for the Express Checkout lane. I was pleased that only one customer was in line ahead of me. For some reason, one of his items failed to register on the electronic scanner. So the clerk grabbed her microphone and called for a price check over the store's intercom system. The customer told the register clerk, "I'm sure the price of that item was $1.69." But the clerk only smiled as two more customers moved into the line behind me.

The first customer, feeling guilty about holding up the growing line, restated his certainty as to the price. The register clerk said, "I'm sure you're right, but the price clerk will only take a minute." By the time another employee walked up to the register and said "$1.69," a total of seven customers were standing in the express line. The register clerk apologized for the delay, quickly rang up the sale, and the obviously frustrated customer bolted out the door.

Do you think the clerk intentionally wanted to hold up the line and frustrate seven customers? Do you really think she did not believe what the customer told her? What do you think the customer thought when the price check confirmed what he had been saying all along? Does it make sense to enforce policies that show a distrust both of the competence of register clerks and of the integrity of customers? Why does this scene happen thousands of times every day all across America? Because good, well-intentioned companies, just like this supermarket, allow policies and procedures to smother common sense. An embarrassed register employee forced into nonproductivity, seven frustrated customers waiting in the so-called Express Checkout lane, another employee taken away from his regular job to roam the store searching for one item, all over a whopping $1.69. And the customer knew the exact price all along! Pretty amazing, yet all too common.

We continue to focus far too much attention on creating checks and balances that attempt to control the incredibly few people in our organizations who might try to beat or exploit the system at the expense of the many who will not. That is a primary purpose of policies and procedures—to control the exceptions. Yet in the attempt to control the one or two percent (instead of getting rid of them), we smother the common sense of the 98 percent who, when they love their work, are trustworthy and ethical.

It is popular today to join the bandwagon of consultants and business writers who proclaim that we should "smash all bureaucracy." But we should be very careful about following their advice to totally eliminate organizational bureaucracy. Without some minimal set of guidelines, some simple system of checks and balances, anarchy could rein. We must not turn a strength (controls) into a weakness by creating bloated policies and procedures. But we must keep the need to maintain some reasonable boundaries well below the point of choking off anything that remotely resembles initiative and individual freedom. Remember, even God issued only ten commandments.

Our goal should not be to completely eliminate bureaucracy but to severely limit its confining scope. We must allow our people the opportunity to use their own common sense, to assess a situation, and then to act in the company's best interests. The key question should be how *little* control is necessary, not how *much* control is necessary. If you are afraid to allow your employees freedom from bureaucracy, then why are they still with your company? To invigorate initiative and productivity, you must create an environment that allows your people to hustle.

Encourage Challenges to the Status Quo

Francis "Buck" Rodgers, the legendary former marketing head of IBM, believes that one of the major causes of poor productivity in business is the large number of people who lack the guts to challenge the status quo. Even when they have the intelligence to challenge it, they are often reluctant to do so because of the potential consequences of bucking the system. How many times have we seen one of our colleagues get into trouble because he took an unpopular stand, asked a tough question, or challenged an assumption? How often can we be verbally or nonverbally rebuffed by senior managers before we begin to keep our opinions to ourselves?

To build commitment, managers must openly encourage, even reward, employees with the guts to challenge the system. There is an old expression that goes "If we only do what we've always done, we'll only get what we've always got." With greater demands for quality, efficiency, and service, it is mandatory that we constantly look for ways to improve our current systems, services, and products. We must encourage everyone, from the front line on up, to question "the way things are done around here." The worst thing any of us can do is to promote and protect a system that fails to challenge the status quo.

Managers must constantly fight the urge to surround themselves with yes-people. Yes-people are men and women who always tell their boss exactly what they think the boss wants to hear. They rarely say anything in front of the boss that would appear to contradict the "company line" or that would in any way look as if they disagree with the manager. Managers who surround themselves with yes-people fail to realize one critical point relevant to today's razor-thin management ranks: If you surround yourself with yes-people, then either you or they are redundant!

Today's best managers go beyond just asking people to speak up; they demand it. They understand the absolute necessity of getting everybody involved in finding ways to improve the business, even to the point of challenging its very foundations. The winning philosophy of Lewis Platt, CEO of the innovative and hugely profitable Hewlett-Packard Company, is to "kill your business while it's still working." And Michael Eisner, CEO of the Disney Corporation, believes that "Whether you're in the business of making cellular phones or computer software . . . or Magic Kingdoms, there's always a better way to do it. Each new initiative should carry the element of the untried."

Challenges to the status quo need not be painful. They begin with a universal recognition that whatever is done today will not be good enough to succeed tomorrow. One plant manager drives home this philosophy by entering his plant each day and asking every station "what records did you break yesterday, because if you didn't break any records, you're still using old methods." We must actively involve all employees in constantly creating brand-new solutions to the brand-new problems we face every day. As a nationally respected human resources executive, Wayne Saunders, loves to say, "All employees come equipped with a brain—at no extra charge!" Engaging those brains in finding new, better, more efficient and more profitable ways to grow a business can only be accomplished through a culture that actively encourages all employees to challenge the status quo.

Give Everyone Input Into Firing the Right Customers

Now that got your attention, didn't it? Imagine allowing your employees to fire customers. Preposterous, isn't it? Absolutely out of the question. We need every customer we can get our hands on, don't we? The customer is king! Then why do so many of us fire customers every day without giving it a second thought?

Retailers "fire" shoplifters every day. They don't need or want that kind of customer, so they're fired! Restaurants "fire" customers who use profanity or openly insult their servers. They don't want that kind of customer, so they're fired! Manufacturers "fire" customers who are perpetually late with payments or who are unreasonably demanding. They don't need that kind of customer, so they're fired! Educators "fire" (dismiss) customers (students) for everything from vandalism and violence to drugs and weapons possession. They don't need that kind of customer, so they're fired!

The concept of firing customers—*any* customer—is still upsetting to most executives and managers. It is tough to accept the reality that, yes, there are some customers, even long-term customers, who should be fired. The overwhelming majority of all customers are decent, honorable people. But, ask yourself this question: Do you have any current customers who are so irritating, irrational, or impossible to please that they cost you and your employees more time, energy, and money than they are worth?" If you answered yes, then consider this: Your competitors may have sent them to you! SEND THEM BACK—NOW!

Please do not misunderstand what I have been saying to mean that anyone should have the right to fire any customer at any time. Rather, imagine the commitment you would receive from your frontline employees if they knew that instead of having constantly to put up with the rudeness, profanity, or insults hurled by a totally irrational, impossible-to-please customer, they can come to you and, with solid reason, suggest that that customer be fired!

This one act alone combines every principle in this book. By allowing an employee the right to suggest that a customer be fired, you have captured the heart of that employee, opened communication on the critically important issue of customer service standards, demonstrated that the employee is a real partner in the business, and driven learning in your customer relations philosophy. The ultimate testimonial in getting your employees to fall and stay in love with your company is the degree to which you encourage their input into firing the right customers.

Best Practices

Here are twenty-two examples of how companies emancipate the action of their employees:

1. "Miztakes Happen."

From its founding, the Hewlett-Packard Company, the computer manufacturer, has encouraged innovation, risk taking, and the freedom to fail honorably. Included in its principles of operation, called "The H-P Way," is this statement: "We (all H-P employees) reserve the right to make mistakes."

2. "Perverse Pride."

Every Saturday in Bentonville, Arkansas, Wal-Mart Stores, the world's largest retailer, gathers together about 300 store managers and corporate staff in Walton Hall to celebrate the company's top twenty-five stores and to work on the bottom twenty-five stores. What sets this meeting apart from other retailer meetings is the almost perverse pride Wal-Mart takes in proudly announcing its mistakes and how it intends to correct them. Lesson: You cannot become one of the world's most profitable and best-run companies by squelching the freedom to fail and try again.

3. "Jail Break."

Great organizations understand that the freedom to fail and try again applies both to the operations and to customer service. One vice president at Alagasco, the Alabama natural gas distributor, in an effort to transform a slow-moving, customer-unfriendly bureaucracy into a fast, customer-friendly service, distributed to all his employees cards inscribed with the words "Get out of jail, free!" When employees make mistakes in their attempts to deliver outstanding service, they go to the vice president, discuss what they have learned from the experience, turn in their cards, and are forgiven. Then, before they leave, the vice president hands them another "Get out of jail, free!" card to be used later. This initiative spurred a tremendous turnaround in the quality of service delivery to Alagasco customers.

4. "SEEK FORGIVENESS, NOT PERMISSION."

MCI became a telecommunications giant not through playing it safe and never making mistakes but by building a culture that thrived on action. As one executive likes to say, "We at MCI don't shoot people who make mistakes; we shoot people who don't take risks."

5. "RULE #1."

One of the simplest and most powerful examples of emancipation from bureaucracy is found at Nordstrom, the Seattle-based department store chain. Its world-renowned levels of customer service are created through what it calls the Nordstrom Rules. Here are the rules in their entirety. "Rule #1: Use your good judgment in all situations. There will be no additional rules." That's it. No double-volume 265-page policy guidelines, but a simple seven-word philosophy that inspires industry-leading sales and service.

6. "ROLE #1."

Harry Quadracci, president of the hugely successful printing company Quad/Graphics, says that his #1 role is that of "main disorganizer." He constantly looks for ways to break up what is already working well and challenges everyone to find even better ways to produce their magazines. Does he walk his talk? Would you sell your proprietary, industry-leading software and manufacturing techniques to your direct competition? Quadracci does, so that his company is always pushing to become better and better.

7. "Don't Stop at Nothin'."

The entire 240-person sales staff at American Express Travel Related Services are telecommuters. They excel at minimizing unnecessary bureaucracy through their "Work anywhere, anytime—as long as it's not in the office" philosophy. Yet they are all connected through groupware, telephones, and cellular networks. Sales staff even receive daily cheerleading messages from the boss like "THINK BIG. THINK GIGANTIC. THINK HUMONGOUS. THINK ABSOLUTELY ASTRONOMICAL. DON'T STOP AT NOTHIN'."[2]

8. "Stick Your Neck Out!"

To encourage risk taking and challenges to the status quo, the candy and food manufacturer Hershey Foods distributes annual awards to those individuals with the guts to "buck the system" and the "willingness to stand the heat for an idea they really believe in." They are called the "Exalted Order of the Extended Neck" awards. Just imagine the creative, cutting-edge ideas permeating the Hershey facilities as the result of such forward-thinking recognition.

9. "Do the Right Thing."

Alex Dillard, executive vice president of Dillard Department Stores, is adamant that his store managers do the right thing with their merchandise. Dillard understands that a store manager understands his or her customers far better than anyone at corporate headquarters. So when he visits his 230 stores, he relentlessly encourages the store managers to locate merchandise where it will best sell and to not just blindly follow the corporate recommendations. Through emancipating the action of its store managers, Dillard continues to be a profitable industry leader.

[2]*Business Week*, June 26, 1995, p. 104.

10. "15% RULE."

Employees at Minnesota Mining and Manufacturing (3M) are allowed to spend up to 15 percent of their time on non-approved "bootleg" projects that they believe have potential for the company. They use their freedom to experiment, do research, build consensus among their colleagues on their ideas, and find internal funding.

11. "COWABUNGA, DUDE."

The office of Ron McDougall, president of the Brinker International restaurant chain, is filled with cow bric-a-brac, including cowbells and ceramic cow lamps. Why? He is encouraging everyone in the company to challenge the status quo, to seek out and destroy any sacred cows that eat away at productivity and profits. The project's code name is, you guessed it, "Cowabunga."

12. "THINK SMALL."

To minimize bureaucracy and emancipate action throughout his 215,000-employee international conglomerate, CEO Percy Barnevik of the Zurich-based ABB Asea Brown Boveri created 5,000 separate profit centers, each with its own profit sheet, while shrinking headquarters staff to 10 percent of its original size. Profit centers average no more than fifty people. Through thinking small, Barnevik has created a highly responsive, largely nonbureaucratic international organization.

13. "RING IT UP."

The Target Department Stores fight bureaucracy and emancipate the action of their cashiers. Whenever there is a question about the price of an item at checkout, cashiers are trained to ask customers if they remember the price. If the customer's price sounds reasonable to the cashier, she rings it up. No price checks, no management OK's. Target sets the pace in recognizing that clerks have brains and customers can be trusted.

14. "NEVER SAY NO."

All sales associates with Parisian's department stores are taught that the only person who can say no to a customer is the store manager. That is quite a different philosophy considering that most companies train for the exceptions, making it easy for associates to say no ("It's against policy," "I'll have to check on it"). Through a "never say no" culture that emancipates the action of all customer-contact associates, Parisian's liberates its associates to live by its first rule: Never let a customer leave unhappy.

15. "THE $100 MISTAKE."

To encourage employees to admit their mistakes before they become monster problems and to encourage risk taking, Steve Ettridge, president of Temps and Company, the Washington, D.C., temporary employment service, offers $100 in cash each quarter to employees who admit mistakes. He knows that promoting a culture that allows people the freedom to fail while quickly admitting and resolving their mistakes saves thousands of dollars annually in wasted time, upset clients, and lost productivity.

16. "THE $500 IMPROVEMENT."

At the Dana Corporation's Toledo plant, employees are allowed to spend $500 per project to improve efficiencies without management approval. More than 80 percent of the improvements are made without the plant manager even knowing about them.

17. "THE $2,000 GRANT."

The Ritz-Carlton Hotel Company emancipates the action of its frontline staff to the tune of $2,000. How? Any employee can do anything he or she needs to do to rectify a guest's complaint on the spot for up to $2,000, no questions asked! Sound crazy? Either an organization trusts the judgment of its people or it doesn't. How much does your company allow frontline staff to invest in satisfying a customer?

18. "Travel Arrangements Courtesy of Our Shareholders."

Corporate travel policies can be a confusing, time-consuming, and bureaucratic nightmare. AT&T eliminated a bunch of company travel restrictions and now lives by the corporate travel statement to "use your good judgment always keeping the shareholders in mind." What a wonderful way to remind all travelers that, ultimately, their travel is being subsidized by the shareholders.[3]

19. "No Messenger Rule."

To encourage teams to take more initiative, Boeing, the Seattle-based airplane manufacturer, has a "no messenger" rule. Team members must make decisions on the spot; they cannot run around looking for a boss to make the decision. Through emancipating the action of its employees, Boeing was able to build its new 777 passenger jet with fewer than one-half the design glitches of any earlier jet program.

20. "Lightly Scrambled, Please."

Doug Bergum, founder and CEO of Great Plains Software, the Fargo, North Dakota, accounting software firm, walked onstage during one of the company's annual dealer conferences and in great detail discussed the mistakes he had made in prematurely bringing a software upgrade to market. He then proceeded to smash three fresh eggs on his forehead. Is Bergum "lightly scrambled"? I think not. Rather, he is a great example of the new breed of leader who can humbly admit that he may not be perfect, but feel that's OK because we all make mistakes, can learn from them and even laugh about them, but then get on with it!

21. "Mr. Customer, You're Fired!"

Today's most progressive companies allow employees direct input into whether to keep or fire customers. When

[3]*Fortune*, January 24, 1994, p. 69.

service staff members of Sewell Motors, the Dallas-based car dealership, come to President Carl Sewell with a recommendation to fire the customer, he often asks them to try again to please the customer. Yet sometimes, after they have taken extraordinary measures to attempt to satisfy a customer, Sewell accepts their recommendation. He has been known to call the customer himself and say, "Mr./Ms. Customer, we choose not to service your car anymore." And in his final display of the world-class service his company is known for, Sewell then says to the customer, "Here are the names and addresses of three of our competitors. *Which competitor would you like us to drive your car to?*"

22. "EMPLOYEES ARE #1."

Herb Kelleher, CEO of Southwest Airlines, will not cave in to customers who abuse, insult, or intimidate his people. Kelleher contends that Southwest does not need this kind of customer. Even more important, he recognizes the incredibly deflating message it would send to his employees if he sided with an abusive customer while ignoring the rights and dignity of his own staff. Imagine the level of commitment that emanates from such a willingness to fire the right customer!

Action Ideas: How to Get On With It!

1. Challenge your team to come up with one idea a month that is so radical it would shock even Howard Stern.

2. Create with your staff a "Top Ten" list of how management gets in the way of progress. Immediately find ways to minimize or eliminate each item.

3. Encourage employees to admit mistakes and share them with others. Always ask them what they will do differently the next time they face the same situation.

4. Give each of your employees a "magic wand" to wave over one customer they would like to see disappear. Ask for

ideas on how to better handle the customer, or begin building a case for firing the customer.

5. Organize a "Page-a-Week" cross-functional team whose sole responsibility is to eliminate at least one page a week from the operations manual.

6. Hold a bureaucracy bomb party that blows up outdated procedures and policies.

7. End every staff meeting with the phrase "Just do it!"

8. Select two actions a month that no longer require your approval or sign-off. Share with your staff.

9. Ask your boss to share with you what procedures and policies drive her crazy, then volunteer to help find ways to change them.

Three of the Best: The Home Depot, *St. Petersburg Times*, Southwest Airlines

This book would be incomplete without examples of how companies combine the five principles into a living, breathing positive work culture. The following case studies examine how three companies have created environments brimming with highly committed and motivated people. I chose these companies because (1) they represent radically different industries (retailing, newspaper publishing, and airline transportation), (2) they have a long track record of financial success, and (3) they are known for their positive employee practices and their ability to inspire and motivate the people who work for them.

No organization is perfect. The three companies presented here would be the first to admit that they are far from perfect. Yet each represents a magnificent model for what can be accomplished when managers live by the principles advanced in this book.

These case studies were drawn from intensive research, on-site visits, interviews, and telephone conversations with multiple company employees. Every attempt has been made to paint a fair and accurate picture of the work environment within each organization.

The differences you will see in their approaches are staggering, but the results are always the same. In their own style, in their own way, The Home Depot, the *St. Petersburg Times*, and Southwest Airlines are all models of how to get employees to fall and stay in love with our companies.

The Home Depot: There's No Place Like Home!

The Home Depot's service philosophy is "every customer must be treated like your mother, your father, your sister, or your brother." Call the headquarters office and the voice message system answers "Thank you for calling The Home Depot *Store Support Center!*" On periodic Wednesdays throughout the year, all headquarters, district, and division employees work in the stores (while a minuscule staff remains at headquarters to answer the phones). Over 80 percent of Home Depot's store employees are *full-time,* and there are no minimum wagers anywhere. Their CEO advises: "If you want a *job,* go someplace else; but if you want a *career,* stay with us." The company believes that "a business enterprise is, first and foremost, a social organization. It is not a collection of real estate, merchandise inventories, and computer networks. It is a highly diverse group of people who each need to be respected for the unique and honorable roles they can contribute to a broad and worthwhile corporate mission."

There's no place like Home!

Founded in 1978 as a high-service, low-price home improvement store, The Home Depot has exploded into a $12.5 billion company. Co-founders Bernie Marcus, CEO, and Arthur Blank, president, head an organization of 80,000 committed employees who serve customers from 364 store locations across thirty states and three Canadian provinces. David Glass, CEO of Wal-Mart, says, "They're running the best retail organization in America today."

Even more than for its magnificent growth and spectacular financial success, The Home Depot is most widely admired for having a corporate culture that inspires employee commitment and enthusiasm. Following some recent soul-searching by current employees who wondered how they could tell new employees about this culture, The Home Depot drafted the following credo, which appears in every new employee information packet.

The Home Depot Culture is about people—
caring human beings who •••
••• value our customers
••• respect fellow associates
••• treat our vendors as partners
••• love what they do
••• feel good about themselves
••• are allowed to make mistakes,
learn from them, and move on
••• are creative and have
an entrepreneurial spirit
••• know they can make a difference
••• ask questions and suggest new ways
••• welcome change

People. Caring human beings. Value and respect. Love. Learning from mistakes. Being creative and entrepreneurial. Making a difference. Welcoming change. These are the cornerstone values of The Home Depot culture. Bernie and Arthur (yes, they insist that everyone call them by their first names) understand that if a company wants to inspire a passionate commitment to taking care of customers, it must first start with an equally passionate commitment to taking care of its people. Live the passion and success follows. How do they know this works? How about nine consecutive years of record earnings and profits, becoming the largest home improvement company in the country, and twice winning *Fortune* magazine's Most Admired Retailer in the Country award?

Treating People Right

Don Singletary, The Home Depot's vice president of employee relations, believes that the success of their culture rests on three key elements. First, at the very core of the culture is a never-ending effort to treat people right. Second is a passionate commitment to letting everyone become an owner and to making the store more than just a place to come to work. Third is a dedication to creating an atmosphere of family that extends beyond their employees and into their communities.

Beyond offering traditional employee benefits, The Home Depot demonstrates its commitment to treating people right through a wide range of progressive programs that include:

- Outstanding medical and dental plans
- A dollar-for-dollar matching fund program for employee donations to their favorite charities or causes
- Up to six months of unpaid leave to take care of pressing family problems
- Adoption assistance programs
- Strong minority hiring and career tracking programs
- Diversity training programs that help employees understand the positive advantages of having a diverse workforce
- Ethics workshops for senior and middle management

Further, The Home Depot truly sets itself apart from 99.9 percent of other retailers through a compensation system that pays employees as partners and treats them as adults. Here is an overview of its approach.

1. All store employees work on a straight salary basis. There are no hourly or commission pay structures.
2. There are no minimum wage employees anywhere in the company. Everyone is paid a very good wage above the minimum wage.
3. More than 80 percent of all store employees work full-time. The reverse ratio (80 percent part-time) is closer to the norm in other retail operations.
4. Employees are offered stock instead of traditional merchandise discounts. Think about it: How many times would an employee retile a bathroom because of a 20 percent employee discount?

5. Employees are paid by experience, not by job title. Since there are no set pay scales, an electrician with twenty-five years' experience will be paid more than an electrician with three years' experience.

The result of such progressive compensation policies is a culture brimming with enthusiastic, long-term-thinking business partners. Also, consider the customer's viewpoint. Would you rather be served by a part-time employee working for a monthly commission or promotional moneys based on sales volume (whether you need the stuff or not) or a salaried, full-time employee interested in the company's long-term performance? By treating employees right, The Home Depot can be very selective about the people it hires.

There may be no other company in the world with a stronger commitment to encouraging every employee to become an owner than The Home Depot. Virtually all employees are eligible for stock purchase incentives. Assistant store managers and higher receive stock options—except for Bernie and Arthur, who stopped receiving stock options years ago because they believe they already have enough and do not want to appear greedy. All other full-timers receive 7 percent of their annual salaries in stock, and twice a year can buy company stock at a discount on the market price. Walk through any store and you will see every employee (including visiting headquarters people) wearing the trademark personalized bright orange aprons emblazoned with the words "Hi, I'm [first name], a Home Depot stockholder. Let me help you."

The Home Depot strives to be more than just another place to work. Its decentralized management structure encourages the innovation and entrepreneurial spirit so vital to its success. Mavericks abound within this structure, in which management proudly proclaims that it probably makes more mistakes per square foot than any retailer in the country, but also has more successes per square foot than any other retailer. It believes that "companies are not entrepreneurial, individuals are" and that "it is easier to correct a failed experiment than to develop and then propagate a creative idea that works." The place is filled with employees experimenting and challenging management without fear of demotion or reprisal. This place also believes that everyone can make a difference and that work should be fun. Sour faces only indicate some store leadership problem, which is immediately addressed and corrected.

Home Depot's Extended Family

Looking upon local communities as part of an extended family is a powerful driving force at The Home Depot. Its history is filled with heartwarming stories of how employees came to the assistance of their extended community family. Orange, Connecticut, store manager Leighton Royster, on receiving a phone call from a house-bound citizen unable to maneuver her wheelchair down her front steps, donated all the materials and labor needed to construct a ramp. He seized an opportunity to help a neighbor and to teach store associates how to build a deck and ramp. After tornadoes ripped through the town of DeSoto, Texas, employees from the nearby Duncanville store drove trucks filled with free lumber, hammers, gloves, and plastic sheeting to help cover the citizens' damaged roofs and windows before the next wave of bad weather struck. After the bombing in Oklahoma City, an assistant store manager knew that relief workers would need lumber and supports to shore up the badly damaged federal building. On his own initiative, he personally loaded and delivered two trucks of lumber, no checkoff needed.

The ethics by which The Home Depot lives was poignantly illustrated during its relief efforts following Hurricane Andrew. The CFO told all South Florida store managers to "do what you've got to do and we'll take care of the numbers later." Headquarters immediately issued a "no profit policy—no price increase policy" on lumber sold, even as suppliers were increasing their prices up to 40 percent. Much of Home Depot's lumber was sold at a loss. Similar approaches were taken during California's forest fires, the floods in the Midwest, and other natural disasters. But The Home Depot's community efforts reach far beyond responding to catastrophes.

"Team Depot" is the company's primary ongoing community volunteer effort; it consists of two key areas. First is "Habitat for Humanity," in which donated materials and labor help build housing via the nationwide "Paint the Town" programs and the "Christmas in April" projects, which repair homes all across the country for the elderly, disabled, and poor. The second major area of community focus is the "Children at Risk" programs such as "If I Had a Hammer," which teaches elementary school children how to use tools.

The Home Depot's ethics extend to an aggressively pushed policy of "Do not let customers overspend." Bernie and Arthur are truly proud of the stories they hear about customers who spent only $4 to $5 on what they really needed versus $150 on what they didn't. Why? Mess with the customer's money only once, they believe, and you risk losing that customer forever. The average customer spends only about $40 per visit, but drops in more than thirty times a year!

How could you not fall in love with a company that takes such strong ethical stands respecting its employees, the community, and its customers?

Open Communication and Constant Learning

The Home Depot focuses tremendous time and energy on keeping the communication channels open in its rapidly growing organization. Most vice presidents spend only a half day a week in their offices; they are always in the store talking with employees and customers. They ask employees "How do you like working here?" and "What are we doing that helps?" and "How are we getting in your way?" and "What do we need to do differently?" An estimated 60 percent to 80 percent of *all* merchandising changes at The Home Depot have come from in-store employees. The VPs also get face-to-face, real-time feedback from customers who tell them how they perceive the shopping experience and if the store is stocking the merchandise they want.

It would be a grand oversight not to mention the now-famous quarterly "Breakfast With Bernie and Arthur" live-via-satellite store meetings. These 6:30 A.M. Sunday morning quasi-revival-type telecasts attract the voluntary participation of over 95 percent of company employees. (OK, there's peer pressure to attend, but still, over 95 percent!) Amid store associates cheering and yoo-hooing, the big guys review company operations and numbers, discuss new happenings, and make these meetings come alive through answering questions from around the country live on this interactive linkup. They are now testing an "On the Road With Bernie and Arthur" program in which large numbers of employees get the chance to meet them in the same room. (Informally, these are known as "The Big Hoopla.") Store managers also hold monthly "All Store Meetings" featuring reviews of company and store financials, product knowledge training, and recognition and awards presentations.There are no pretensions at The Home Depot. During my first visit to company headquarters, while I waited in the main lobby, a man burst through a doorway headed out of the office. Just as he stepped by the front desk, the receptionist smiled and shouted "Hello, Bernie!" Now, how often would a similar scene occur in a Fortune 500 or most any headquarters office? In 96.96 percent (my unofficial intuitive estimate) of the reception areas in America, anything short of the receptionist calling the CEO "Mr." and "Sir" is still a miracle. But what else can you say to a guy who's orange store apron reads "Hi. My name is Bernie"?

Learning at The Home Depot starts at the top. Bernie requires the board of directors to make ten unannounced store visits per quarter to talk with employees and customers. This drives board member learning about what is really happening in the stores and speeds up board decision making. There may not be another board of directors in America required to take such an active part in learning the business of their business. Bernie and Arthur also walk the talk of the importance of training and learning. They both spend one day a month in leading new store manager training programs and preaching their gospel of service.

The Home Depot offers a full range of training programs for employees, particularly in product knowledge. The first week in the store, all new hires must complete a product knowledge workbook on their department. Within thirty days of being hired, they must complete the product knowledge books for adjacent departments. All employees are encouraged to complete all product knowledge books and be awarded the "Product Knowledge Master" award, a badge designed as a cap and gown for their aprons.

The Home Depot is a magnificent example of a people-focused culture. Through both progressive and aggressive programs, they show us how to win through an unrelenting focus on the people side of business. If you are still uncertain as to the importance of such an approach, let me tell you of the caption under a huge western roundup painting hanging in Bernie's office. The caption reads, "If you don't make dust, you eat dust." The Home Depot's people-focused approach is making its competitors chew a lot of dust!

Ahh, there *is* no place like (The) Home!

The *St. Petersburg Times:* An Environment That Cares

How many companies do you know of in which more than 89 percent of the employees would say it was not just a "nice" place to work, or even a "good" place to work, but that it was a *"great"* place to work? How many companies do you know of that contribute to an employee's retirement fund whether or not the employee contributes to it in a given year? How many companies do you know of that have a special quarterly cost of living adjustment paid out in cash? The only one I know of is the *St. Petersburg* (Florida) *Times* newspaper.

Founded in 1894 by Nelson Poynter, the *St. Petersburg Times* is a multiple-Pulitzer-Prize-winning newspaper that has grown to be the second largest newspaper in Florida, trailing only the *Miami Herald*. Its total of 3,500 employees (called "staffers") break down into 1,700 full-time and 1,800 part-time staffers, the latter being home delivery, customer service, transportation, and packaging professionals.

Talk to any staffers and you get the feeling that they work for a uniquely different company. Staffers beam with pride over the company's uncompromisingly high standards of journalism. The *Times* treats all stories with the same candor and investigative vigor, and it is not reluctant to run embarrassing stories about itself, its staffers, or even its advertisers. Yet the *Times*'s very high professional standards go hand in hand with promoting a rampant individualism. Traditional business dress is not shunned; rather individual identities are encouraged. The facilities are filled with people of every size, shape, color, and national origin within a culture that exudes "hey, just be yourself." Sound extreme to you? At the *Times*, the only extreme is the extremely fun-filled castigation staffers receive if they are perceived as *not* being themselves.

CEO Andy Barnes is committed to creating an organization for life, one that inspires all employees to spend their entire careers at the *Times*. At press time, the paper had ninety-four active staffers and more than 115 retirees with over twenty-five years' tenure. Such amazing loyalty results in part from Barnes's often repeated and compelling mission statement: "The *Times* makes a profit to print a newspaper. We do not print a newspaper to make a profit."

Benefits and Services

Few organizations are more sincerely dedicated to the current and future well-being of their employees than the *Times* is. The benefits and services offered to staffers read like a roll call of today's most progressive employee practices. They include:

- Job sharing, split shifts, and flextime programs
- Expectant parent programs
- Adoption assistance
- Work and family seminars on parenting skills and elder care in which employee spouses and children are welcome and encouraged to attend
- "Summer Care Fairs" that acquaint staffers with summer care options for children
- A "Bearly Sick" program, with a teddy bear as a mascot, that offers alternative day care at a neighborhood

hospital for children between the ages of eight weeks and fourteen years who are too ill to be at regular day care facilities or who have a minor illness

- Parental leave for up to one year after a child is born (two dads have taken the full year)
- Vacation flexibility to take a day when it is needed, even a day at a time
- For full-timers, a combination of ten national holidays and personal leave days above and beyond their accrued vacation time
- An on-staff family specialist who assists staffers with their dependent care needs

Is it any wonder that the *Times* is a multiple winner of *Working Mother* magazine's 100 Best Companies in America award? At last count, it has been listed four years in a row.

Pride abounds among staffers who discuss the millions of dollars the *Times* annually invests in their central Gulf Coast communities. The *Times* sponsors or co-sponsors everything from baby shows and sporting events to a "Newspapers in Education" program that donates papers to schools, while at the same time lavishly supporting local theater, arts, and a multitude of cultural events. The *Times* captures the hearts of both its staffers and readers through active leadership in United Way campaigns and dozens of other programs that support the greater Tampa Bay social services.

Such community and family pride spills over into the *Times'* many company celebrations and family get-togethers. Chief among the fun events is the annual "Company Party" that all staffers and their families are invited to attend. In recent years, the "Company Party" has hosted everything from plant tours to an outdoor games and crafts festival. One year it featured a huge pool party. This past year's attendance was more than 4,000 staffers and retirees (oh yes, retirees are considered part of the family, too).

Internal Communications

What would a newspaper be without a strong internal communications system? Not a great one, that's for sure. The

Times puts considerable effort into maintaining open communication channels among all levels of employees. Most evident is the biweekly internal newsletter called *Times Talk* that focuses on any relevant company happenings. One recent issue included articles on the prestigious recycling award the company received for using 100 percent soybean oil–based ink instead of petroleum-based ink; a midyear company profits summary; its diversity training program; the winners of a football ticket giveaway; the settlement of a class action suit against the company; and the power of compounding in saving for retirement. Further, each issue lists the births of children and grandchildren to staffers, extends sympathy on the deaths of staffer family members, offers "get well" wishes to ill staffers, and lists staffer promotions and job transfers.

The *Times* understands the need to use multiple internal communication channels and not to become too dependent on the written word alone. One example is the "Company Forum," a monthly one- to two-hour interactive staff meeting held in all five company facilities spread over the Tampa Bay region. The general manager and communications director, along with various department heads, travel to each site to meet face to face with staffers and engage in lively discussions on everything from operational results and financial statements to coping with organizational stress. During each forum there is also time allotted for sharing "Success Stories," recognizing outstanding individual or group efforts, and openly discussing current news events. Another great communication program is the quarterly training session called the "Orientation Program," in which board members and department heads meet face to face with new hires to discuss the *Times*'s culture and operations.

In addition, this is a company whose benefits structure makes little distinction between what is offered executives and part-time employees; the *Times* has no reserved parking (staffers can either pay for their own spaces in a parking garage across the street from the headquarters or walk the four short blocks from the company lot); gives quarterly cash cost-of-living adjustments to full-time staffers; mandates annual board reviews of all salaries to ensure pay equity across race and gender lines; and offers three retirement plans: a traditional pension plan, a 401k plan in which the company annually contributes to staffer accounts whether the staffer makes a contribution that year or not, and a profit sharing program for anyone who works more than 1,000 hours per year. Would you say that such a company is attempting to build a partnership with all its employees? I would.

Teambuilding and Training

Additionally, the *Times* employs a series of progressive programs to build stronger internal partnerships. One program develops annual departmental goals through a cross-functional team approach headed by a nondepartmental "Team Champion." The Team Champion is responsible for choosing and recruiting team members, organizing the team process, and facilitating the formation of the annual goals for their assigned department. Another program offered other cross-functional teams an opportunity to earn points toward merchandise purchases through generating cost-cutting or revenue-enhancing ideas.

Training is also very important at the *Times*. Managers receive a minimum of four days of training per year, other staffers three days of training per year. The "Professional Development Program" is a one-year management program in which nominated staffers gain valuable exposure to all business areas while being offered career and self-development, including strengths assessment, teambuilding, and presentation skills. More than eighty managers were nominated for the fifteen available openings last year.

Besides offering a wide range of traditional training, the *Times* is relentlessly committed to diversity and diversity training. Diversity training is *very* important at the *Times*. Its goal is to "help individuals learn how to pay attention and raise their levels of comfort with *all* differences . . . the value of seeing others in their fullest dimensions." In short, the *Times* promotes the fundamental concept of respect.

This combination of a powerful mission, world-class benefits for its employees, and a terrific communications system, all swirling inside a culture that loves its profession, liberates the individualism of its staffers, and thrives on its strength of diversity, makes the *St. Petersburg Times* a worthy case study of an environment that cares.

Southwest Airlines: Feel the Spirit of LUV

You begin to feel the spirit the second you enter the front door of Southwest Airlines' headquarters. A huge, open-air three-story lobby is alive with memorabilia of the company's history. Stroll past the welcome area into the long corridors separating offices and you are overwhelmed by the company's celebration of people—a breathtaking array of hundreds of large framed collages holding thousands of photographs of employees celebrating everything from company-sponsored parties and get-togethers, softball teams, and community projects, to Halloween, Easter, and even "Playing Baseball with Nolan Ryan Day." Original employee art, from wall hangings to oil paintings, is skillfully interlaced among the uncountable collages.

Awards are everywhere. Plaques labeled Heroes of the Heart, the Kitty Hawk Award, the Winning Spirit Award, the President's Award, and the Sense of Humor Award (which is, of course, hung upside down) proudly display the names of recipients. There is even a Customer of the Month award.

Throughout the building, employees briskly stride through the hallways toward their appointed duties. The air is filled with smiles and laughter and talk of "heroes and heroines," "hearts and souls," "positively outrageous service," and LUV. The company's three-sentence mission statement is splattered around the building, with its last line proclaiming "Above all, employees will be provided the same concern, respect, and caring attitude within our organization that they are expected to share externally with every . . . customer." Cynics may think they have stumbled onto a make-believe Hollywood studio set and walk around asking themselves "Is this heaven?" No, it's Southwest Airlines.

Perhaps no other company in America has more proudly,

or for a longer period, lived the principles promoted in this book than has Southwest Airlines. What began on June 18, 1971, with ten customers, two bags, and a small group of anxious employees has grown into the nation's sixth-largest airline, with over 18,000 employees and serving forty-five cities across twenty-two states.

A Fun Place to Work

Herb Kelleher, the legendary co-founder and current CEO, president, and chairman of the board, built his company on LUV, which represents the company's home base at Dallas Love Airport, its NYSE stock symbol, and the Southwest spirit. Nourished from headquarters, this spirit extends to the gates and ground crews and eventually into the planes. You are just as likely to participate in a "Guess the Gate Agent's Weight" contest before boarding your plane as you are to hear a flight crew announce, "There may be fifty ways to leave your lover, but there are only six exits from this plane."

The first time most headquarters visitors see the spirit in action is when they enter the People Department (naturally, it's not called anything boring like "Personnel" or even "Human Resources"). As you walk through the door just off the main lobby, your senses are overloaded with sights and sounds and smells. A large plaque with the department's mission statement, personally autographed by all department employees, is prominently displayed on the wall. Several plastic Southwest airplane blow-up toys hang from the ceiling. Dozens of pictures (Kodak must also LUV this place) in large frames show People Department employees celebrating Halloween parties, support of Ronald McDonald houses, fund-raisers, the Friday afternoon employee "bashes," and company magazine ads. A ceiling-mounted TV monitor runs a continuous-loop tape of a combination of television commercials, employee interviews on what Southwest means to them, and dozens of outtakes from company celebrations (Herb as a wrestler, St. Patrick's Day parties, and so on). You definitely get the feeling that this group likes to have fun. The tantalizing aroma from the circus-style popcorn machine invites you to buy a 10-cent bag, with proceeds going to the company's "Catastrophic Fund" to assist employees in financial need.

One wall of the People Department displays a large array of brightly colored cards. Each color represents a different job classification at Southwest. The cards briefly outline the requirements of that job. On the top of every card are three red hearts (LUV again) with the phrase "People—the Heart of Southwest Airlines." The first sentence of every card reads "If you're a highly motivated, people-oriented, outgoing, energetic individual who wants to become part of a winning airline team—you've come to the right place." Every card has three major sections: "Make a difference," a general description of the duties of that job; "What it takes," an overview of the minimum requirements for the job; and "Welcome Aboard," the process after selection, including a job training overview. At the bottom of every card, centered and in bold letters, is the phrase "Reach for the Sky—Join the Southwest Airlines team!" You feel the spirit even through these multicolored, bookmark-size job descriptions.

The Spirit of Service

Nowhere is the spirit of LUV more alive than in the booklet every new employee receives entitled *The Book on Service— What positively outrageous service looks like at Southwest Airlines.* Written by Fawn Boyd of the People Department and Monica Van Slate of the Executive Office, this eighty-plus-page book summarizes the spirit of Southwest through sharing dozens of wonderful examples of employees delivering positively outrageous service (POS in Southwest lingo) in chapters like "Courtesy," "Comfort," "The Extra Mile," "Fun," and "Over the Top." They write that the birth of Southwest combined three visions: "changing our [America's] approach to air transportation, fighting for its independence among the 'giants,' and believing that a little bit of LUV and magic really can make dreams come true." The last line of the book reads: "It's your Company; your success; your future—thanks for always giving your best!!"

Why focus so much on the Southwest spirit? Because, according to the company, everything good that has happened to Southwest Airlines has come from capturing the hearts of its employees. As *The Book on Service* says, "today, the dream is still alive, and corporate America is still amazed. Perhaps they haven't yet figured out that the key to our success is actually very, very simple. It's in our heart—literally, in the 12,000+ hearts that beat every day in tune to the music of Southwest Airlines." Herb (everybody calls him Herb) and his co-founder, Rollin King, created a vision that continues today—simple in design, innovative in operation, and unsurpassed in spirit. The results speak for themselves—twenty-two consecutive years of profits in an industry swimming in red ink, the highest productivity per employee in the industry, 160,000 applications for employment last year, incredibly low turnover, and receipt of the prestigious Department of Transportation's "Triple Crown" award for three consecutive years honoring the industry's highest ratings for on-time performance, baggage handling, and fewest customer complaints. That's the bottom line on LUV at Southwest.

Keeping the Momentum Going

Keeping the momentum going may be the single greatest challenge facing Southwest Airlines. Elizabeth "Liz" Simmons, director of training and development, says that one way Southwest keeps positive momentum going is by aggressively focusing all employees on two issues—the incredible rate of change, and the volatility of the market within the airline industry. Even with the most unionized workforce in the industry, Southwest is considered to have the best union relations through its open communication and partnership-building practices. The best example is the unprecedented ten-year pact between the pilot's union and Southwest based not on the traditional automatic pay raises but on long-term stock incentives. It's no wonder that pilots so often help to clean the interiors of the planes between passenger loadings and volunteer to help scrub down their plane's exteriors on their free time. (Imagine your white-collar management team *voluntarily* scrubbing and waxing the floors of your office!)

One of the most innovative ways Southwest Airlines focuses on keeping the momentum going is through its Culture Committee. Yes, you read that right, a Culture Committee. More than 300 employees from all forty-five locations volunteer to meet *on their own time* to focus on areas such as what the company is doing well, how to keep morale high, how to handle employee suggestions better, and how to improve the operations and the overall company culture.

Here's a sampling of the many other ways in which Southwest keeps the LUV burning bright:

• At the 1994 Annual Chili Cook-off, the pilots presented to Herb a customized Harley-Davidson motorcycle. A few weeks later, the employees had to discipline him because he was riding around the hallways too much.

• Magazine ads feature real Southwest employees.

• Every month, 100 percent of the air in the headquarters building is filtered; the drinking water is constantly recycled and is as pure as bottled water (although Southwest really does not like to brag about it).

• Holiday contests abound, with a best Valentine's Day costume, best decorated Easter egg and Easter bonnet contests, and, of course, Halloween contests. The huge annual Halloween celebration includes opening up headquarters for trick-or-treating by employee family members and local schoolchildren.

• Winners of the "Heroes of the Heart" award, given to behind-the-scenes service champions, are honored by having their department name painted on a designated plane for one year.

• A true open-door policy exists so that when you want to see an executive and he or she is there, you go right in. No one is ever told, "No, you can't see him/her."

• A "New Employee Lunch" is held twice yearly to maintain open communication between executives and new hires. Executives ask such questions as "Is the company doing for you what you thought it would?" "What can we do better?" and "How can we make Southwest a better company?"

- Every employee suggestion receives a personal response within thirty days.

- Key operational numbers, including monthly load factors and quarterly company financials, are shared with all employees.

- The employee phone book is a three-ring binder that begins with a one-page fact sheet on all senior management employees along with their pictures. The fact sheet goes beyond basic data and asks such intriguing questions as "When I relax, I. . . ."

- The "Front Line Forum" is a full-day meeting for a cross-section of employees celebrating at least ten years with the company. Vice presidents give an overview of their areas and then open discussion with questions like "How do you feel about Southwest?" "How can we keep you going, keep you motivated and enthused?" "What has kept you here for ten years?" "What questions can I answer for you?"

- Whenever you see a group of employee pictures that includes a portrait of Herb, his photo is never on top. You will find his picture in the middle of everyone's else's. Herb wants everyone to understand that he is just another employee, a partner in the business.

- After Herb announced a 100 percent company match on employee 401k contributions, the employees gave him a "Thank-You" poster.

- Top managers spend at least one day each quarter working in the field as reservation clerks, ticket agents, and baggage handlers.

- Office employees volunteer to work ground crew shifts on "Black Wednesday," the day before Thanksgiving and one of the toughest days of the year. Last year, Herb worked the midnight shift (11 P.M. to 7 A.M.) to help maintenance with their overnight responsibilities, which include thorough cleaning and waxing of the aircraft.

- To drive learning about the history of Southwest, the company requires all new hires to participate in a headquarters-based scavenger hunt. They receive a list of significant company dates and are told to scour the headquarters hallway memorabilia for the answers. The new hires are even encouraged to corner current employees for the answers.

- Training is a critically important part of keeping the spirit alive. Courses with titles like "The Up and Coming Leader," "Customer-Care Training," and "Front-Line Leadership" abound. All new hires attend a one-day "YSS" program focusing on You—Southwest—Success. A three-day "Leading with Integrity" middle-management training program focuses on two key principles: (1) Each manager is 100 percent accountable for all his or her actions, and (2) each manager is responsible for getting employees whatever they need to be successful.

- The "Walk a Mile Program" allows employees to work for one day a year in another operational area to learn about that area. Travel incentives are offered for overall employee participation.

- To make learning the company financials more fun, Southwest during one twelve-week period mailed every employee a weekly "Quiz Card" that contained a series of questions on the financials. The answers to the questions were listed in the employee newsletter that same week. All employees who recorded and returned all answers were registered to win free travel.

The list of the ways in which Southwest keeps the spirit alive could go on and on. Yet two stories may best illustrate this spirit of LUV. A Chicago toy manufacturer wished to donate hundreds of teddy bears for distribution during the Sunday community meeting following the tragic Oklahoma City bombing. He tried for several days to find a company that would volunteer to transport his donation. Late on Saturday afternoon, someone suggested he call Southwest Airlines. Without hesitation (and without the need for sign-offs or OK's from above), a Southwest manager immediately allocated space on a plane to Chicago, helped load the teddy bears aboard, and made the necessary arrangements for the bears to arrive in Oklahoma City in time for the Sunday community service. Like so many other great companies, Southwest chose not to publicize its participation in yet another special event.

How might a group of employees show their LUV for the company? When fuel prices shot up during the Gulf War, ground employees *voluntarily*—without Herb's or any other top manager's knowledge—began a *payroll deduction program to defray fuel costs*. Now that's LUV, the pure spirit of Southwest Airlines.

From Culture Committees to popcorn machines, from Heroes of the Heart to Customer of the Month, from bosses receiving motorcycles to children receiving teddy bears, to voluntary payroll deductions to defray operational costs, the spirit of LUV shines brightly within Southwest Airlines. Is such LUV contagious? Just ask Pat Janson, a one-year employee of the People Department, who told me, "You don't work here. You become part of it."

Action Plan

Here is a simple two-step approach to use in reenergizing your workplace.

> **Step 1:** Complete the *Fast Start Survey* to help you decide which of the five principles discussed in this book needs the most immediate attention.

> **Step 2:** Turn to the *Action Plan Worksheets* and complete all five exercises beginning with your #1-ranked principle from the *Fast Start Survey*.

Step 1: *Fast Start Survey*

Knowing where to start on the road to getting employees to fall in love with your company is very important. Here is a *Fast Start Survey* to help you decide on which of the five key principles you should begin. Circle one number for each statement. Add the numbers you circled for each principle and record the total in the score space provided.

For each statement, circle the number that best describes your department or organization.

Circle 5 if you strongly agree with the statement.
Circle 4 if you somewhat agree with the statement.
Circle 3 if you are neutral on the statement.
Circle 2 if you somewhat disagree with the statement.
Circle 1 if you strongly disagree with the statement.

Capture the Heart	
1. We have a written vision that is known to all and lived every day.	1 2 3 4 5
2. We seek creative, low-cost ways to balance work and family.	1 2 3 4 5
3. We love to celebrate and find innovative ways to inject fun into the workplace.	1 2 3 4 5
Capture the Heart Score	

Open Communication	
1. It is obvious that management considers internal listening a priority.	1 2 3 4 5
2. Attention is given to using multiple communication channels—more than just using memos and E-mail.	1 2 3 4 5
3. Employees receive feedback in real time (immediate, direct, positive) rather than merely occasional performance appraisals.	1 2 3 4 5
Open Communication Score	

Create Partnerships	
1. There are few if any status barriers between employees (i.e., reserved parking, bonuses only for top management, special benefits).	1 2 3 4 5
2. We actively share financial numbers, ratios, and company performance measures with all employees.	1 2 3 4 5
3. Management visibly serves the frontline, customer-contact employee first (providing tools, resources, and training) before asking the frontline employee to serve management with reports, paperwork, etc.	1 2 3 4 5
Create Partnerships Score	

Drive Learning	
1. We guarantee lifelong employability (rather than lifetime employment) through offering extensive training, cross-training, and work variety.	1 2 3 4 5
2. Special attention is given to creating visible, activity-filled programs that help drive learning through all levels of the organization—up, down, and laterally.	1 2 3 4 5
3. We actively support a philosophy of lifelong learning for our employees that goes beyond focusing only on today's job needs.	1 2 3 4 5
Drive Learning Score	

Emancipate Action	
1. We allow employees the freedom to fail and try again.	1 2 3 4 5
2. Constant attention is given to creating freedom from bureaucracy, unnecessary sign-offs, outdated procedures, and office politics.	1 2 3 4 5
3. All employees are encouraged to openly challenge the status quo to help find better, faster, more profitable ways to serve our customers.	1 2 3 4 5
Emancipate Action Score	

Summary Score: Transfer your scores from each principle into the Score column below. The higher the score is, the more you believe this principle is alive and well in your organization. Rank-order your scores from 1 to 5 (lowest score = 1, highest score = 5) in the Rank column. For example, a score of 20 will rank *lower* than a score of 15.

Principle	Score	Rank
Capture the Heart	_____	_____
Open Communication	_____	_____
Create Partnerships	_____	_____
Drive Learning	_____	_____
Emancipate Action	_____	_____

Where to Begin: Begin with the #1-ranked principle—your lowest score. That's the principle you said is least evident in your organization. Turn to the worksheet for that principle in the next section. Follow the guidelines to create an action plan for that principle. Then, go to your #2-ranked principle and create an action plan for it. Continue to create action plans for all five principles.

Step 2: *Action Plan Worksheets*

Turn to the worksheet for your #1-ranked principle. Follow the guidelines to create an action plan for that principle. Remember to review the *Action Ideas* suggested at the end of each chapter dealing with the five principles to help you build your action plans. Then, go to your #2-ranked principle worksheet and create an action plan for it. Continue the process until you have created an action plan for all five principles.

In three months, assess the action plans and retake the *Fast Start Survey*. Rank the principles and begin the action plan process anew.

Remember, creating an organization brimming with consistently motivated and committed employees demands that you take a consistent and committed approach to meeting their needs.

Capture the Heart Worksheet

Strategies
- Live a compelling vision.
- Balance work and family.
- Celebrate and have fun.

Action Plan Review the *Action Ideas* at the end of Chapter 2. List three *Capture the Heart* actions to implement in your organization. Note *Who* must be involved, *When* to begin, *How* to initiate the plan, and the *Results* expected and obtained.

Action #1 _____	
Who	
When	
How	
Results	
Action #2 _____	
Who	
When	
How	
Results	
Action #3 _____	
Who	
When	
How	
Results	

Open Communication Worksheet

Strategies
- Establish internal listening as a priority.
- Use multiple internal communication channels.
- Encourage two-way interaction.
- Give feedback in real time.

Action Plan   Review the *Action Ideas* at the end of Chapter 3. List three *Open Communication* actions to implement in your organization. Note *Who* must be involved, *When* to begin, *How* to initiate the plan, and the *Results* expected and obtained.

Action #1 _____

Who

When

How

Results

Action #2 _____

Who

When

How

Results

Action #3 _____

Who

When

How

Results

Create Partnerships Worksheet

Strategies
- Squash status barriers.
- Open the company books.
- Pay for performance, not titles.
- Share the bad times as well as the good times.
- Serve the frontline partner first.

Action Plan Review the *Action Ideas* at the end of Chapter 4. List three *Create Partnerships* actions to implement in your organization. Note *Who* must be involved, *When* to begin, *How* to initiate the plan, and the *Results* expected and obtained.

Action #1 _____

Who

When

How

Results

Action #2 _____

Who

When

How

Results

Action #3 _____

Who

When

How

Results

Drive Learning Worksheet

Strategies
- Guarantee employability, not employment.
- Promote visible, action-filled learning.
- Encourage continuous, lifelong learning.

Action Plan Review the *Action Ideas* at the end of Chapter 5. List three *Driving Learning* actions to implement in your organization. Note *Who* must be involved, *When* to begin, *How* to initiate the plan, and the *Results* expected and obtained.

Action #1 _____

Who

When

How

Results

Action #2 _____

Who

When

How

Results

Action #3 _____

Who

When

How

Results

Emancipate Action Worksheet

Strategies
- Allow the freedom to fail and try again.
- Create freedom from bureaucracy.
- Encourage challenges to the status quo.
- Allow all employees input into firing the right customers.

Action Plan   Review the *Action Ideas* at the end of Chapter 6. List three *Emancipate Action* actions to implement in your organization. Note *Who* must be involved, *When* to begin, *How* to initiate the plan, and the *Results* expected and obtained.

Action #1 _____

Who

When

How

Results

Action #2 _____

Who

When

How

Results

Action #3 _____

Who

When

How

Results

Epilogue

The End ... and a New Beginning

Although this is the end of the book, the principles, best practices, and action plans suggested actually represent a new beginning. They are a new beginning for the approaches we must take to inspire the commitment of our employees.

All the principles discussed here are interrelated. No doubt, as you read the best practices you thought that many of them could easily fit under two or more principles. You are absolutely right in thinking this. The five principles certainly do overlap. The key is not to focus on which principles a best practice best fits but rather to use the best practices as guidelines for bringing the principles to life within your organization.

If asked to summarize this book in one sentence, I would quote a powerful line from the legendary Walt Disney, who once said: "You can dream, create, design, and build the most wonderful place in the world . . . but it requires people to make the dream a reality." I hope this book helps make your dream for your business a reality.

Summary List of the Five Principles

Principle #1–Capture the Heart

>   Live a compelling vision.
>   Balance work and family.
>   Celebrate and have fun.

Principle #2–Open Communication

>   Establish internal listening as a priority.
>   Use multiple internal communication channels.
>   Encourage two-way interaction.
>   Give feedback in real time.

Principle #3–Create Partnerships

>   Squash status barriers.
>   Open the company books.
>   Pay for performance, not titles.
>   Share the bad times as well as the good times.
>   Serve the frontline partners first.

Principle #4–Drive Learning

>   Guarantee employability, not employment.
>   Promote visible, action-filled learning.
>   Encourage continuous, lifelong learning.

Principle #5–Emancipate Action

> Allow freedom to fail and try again.
> Create freedom from bureaucracy.
> Encourage challenges to the status quo.
> Give everyone input into firing the right customers.

Alphabetical List of Best Practice Companies

ABB Asea Brown Boveri
A. G. Edwards and Sons
Alagasco
All American Bottling
Allen-Bradley
Allstate Insurance
American Express Travel
    Related Services
Ameritech
AMETEK–Mansfield and
    Green Division
Amy's Ice Cream
Apple Computer
ARES, Inc.
AT&T
Baptist Hospital of Miami
Ben & Jerry's Homemade
Beth Israel Hospital of Boston
The Body Shop

Boeing
Boston Market
Bread Loaf Construction
Brinker International
Burger King Corporation
Chaparral Steel
Charleston Area Medical
    Center
Chef Allen's
Chiat Day
Chick-fil-A Restaurants
Cigna Group Pension
    Division
Conners Communication
Cummins Engines
Cunningham
    Communications
Dahlin Smith White
Dana Corporation

Dean Junior College
  (Franklin, Massachusetts)
Delta Airlines
Dillard Department Stores
Disney Corporation
Domino's Pizza
Donnelly Corporation
DuPont
East Jefferson General
  Hospital
Eaton Corporation
Eckerd Corporation
Essilor of America
Federal Express
First Chicago
First Federal Bank of
  California
First Interstate Bank of
  California
First National Bank of
  Maryland
Florida Forest Products
Galacticomm
Gardener Supply
General Electric
General Motors–Cadillac
  Division
General Motors–Saturn
  Division
Great Plains Software
Harza Engineering
Haworth, Inc.
Herman Miller
Hershey Foods
Hewlett-Packard Company
Hi-Tech Hose
The Home Depot
Home Shopping Network
Honda Motors

Honeywell
Iams Company
Intel Corp.
ipd Co.
John Deere & Company
John Nuveen Co.
Johnsonville Foods
J. P. Morgan
Kwik Kopy
Lancaster Laboratories
Lincoln Electric
Manco, Inc.
McBer and Company
MCI
McCormick & Company
Meredith Publishing
Minnesota Mining and
  Manufacturing (3M)
Mirage Hotel
Motorola
NationsBank
New Hope Communications
Nordstrom
North American Tool and
  Dye
Nucor Steel
Olin Corporation
Open Market
Outback Steakhouse
Owens-Corning Fiberglass
Parisian's
Penn Parking
PepsiCo
Pinellas County (FL) Public
  Schools
Prince Manufacturing
Prospect Associates
Prudential Insurance
Quad/Graphics

Restek
Rhino Foods
Ridgeview Hosiery
Ritz-Carlton Hotel Company
Rodale Press
Rosenbluth Travel
Salem Sportswear
Sandoz Pharmaceuticals
Sequent Computer Systems
Sewell Motor Company
Silicon Graphics
Southwest Airlines
Springfield ReManufacturing
St. Petersburg Times

Stride Rite
Symmetrix, Inc.
Target Department Stores
Tattered Cover Bookstore
Temps and Company
Texas A&M University
Townsend Engineering
University of Texas–Austin
UPS–United Parcel Service
Valeo
Wabash National
Wal-Mart Stores
Wilton Conner Packaging
Winn Dixie Stores
Xerox Corporation

Recommended Readings

Body and Soul: Profits with Principles by Anita Roddick, New York: Crown Publishing Group, 1991. The amazing success story of The Body Shop personal-care products retailer as told by its founder. Wonderful example of a profitable, values-driven company. Compelling discussions on the need for corporations to take the high road in regard to the principles by which they manage people and their business.

Built to Last: Successful Habits of Visionary Companies by James Collins and Jerry Porras, New York: HarperBusiness, 1994. Summarizes a multiyear research investigation on why great companies last. In a word, the key is culture—an almost cultlike environment where employees easily recognize and passionately believe in the company's core values. Intended for readers who wish to study the lessons learned from business giants.

The Customer Comes Second by Hal Rosenbluth and Diane McFerrin Peters, New York: William Morrow and Company, 1992. An engaging, powerful story of how Hal Rosenbluth transformed a small Philadelphia-based travel agency into a billion-dollar international transportation services company through one simple principle—the employees come first. Offers hands-on, creative ways to build a vibrant, profitable work culture.

Danger in the Comfort Zone by Judith Bardwick, New York: AMA-COM, 1995. A poignant discussion of how to help employees overcome the fear of losing their job security (entitlement) while maintaining a focus on earning profit. A caring, yet results-focused approach to business through the eyes of a business-smart psychologist.

The Invisible Assembly Line by Daniel Stamp, New York: AMACOM, 1995. Stamp presents an eight-step process to boost productivity in the new economy. He demonstrates how to align values and vision, generate employee ownership, and bridge organizational and personal learning.

Love and Profit: The Art of Caring Leadership by James Autrey, New York: William Morrow and Company, 1991. A Fortune 500 executive blends prose and poetry in exploring the need for humanness in the pursuit of profit. Autrey takes a close look at how managers must take care of rather than manipulate their employees. Dozens of Autrey's poems about the workplace provide a unique perspective on managing.

A Manager's Guide to the Millennium by Ken Matejka and Richard Dunsing, New York: AMACOM, 1995. Insightful and contemporary discussion of how to recognize meaningful business trends and build an optimal organization. Filled with exercises and self assessments with an excellent game plan for building a "dream team" through inspiring ("hooking") employee commitment to the company vision ("dream").

The New Partnership: Profit by Bringing Out the Best in Your People, Customers, and Yourself by Tom Melohn, Oliver Wright Publications, 1994. Perhaps the most progressive, enlightening inside look at a monstrously successful company this decade. A magnificent behind-the-scenes story of creating a positive people-driven culture through the eyes of the chairman.

The 100 Best Companies to Work For in America by Robert Levering and Milton Moskowitz, New York: Doubleday, 1993. A summary of 100 two-to-three page overviews of (according to the authors) the 100 top companies in America. Interesting explanations of how each company creates its unique culture along such dimensions as pay/benefits and friendliness. Objectively offers both the upside and the downside to each organization profiled.

1001 Ways to Reward Employees by Bob Nelson, New York: Workman Publishing, 1994. Thorough overview of basic reward and motivational incentive programs. Easy to read with an entertaining use of graphics.

The Pursuit of WOW! by Tom Peters, New York: Vintage Books, 1994. Another marvelous book by Peters on how to transform today's companies into tomorrow's winners. His messages continue to restate the obvious—only through empowered, excited, turned-on people can any organization hope to thrive in today's (or tomorrow's) economy. A must-read for progressive thinking businesspeople who want to WOW their customers.

Second to None: How Smart Companies Put People First by Charles Garfield, Burr Ridge, Ill.: Business One Irwin, 1992. An in-depth exploration of how peak performing organizations maintain high levels of teamwork and creativity. Poignant discussions on the new workplace dynamics and how great companies focus on their employees to maintain their winning edge.

SuperMotivation: A Blueprint for Energizing Your Organization From Top to Bottom by Dean Spitzer, New York: AMACOM, 1995. A fresh, no-nonsense look at how to eliminate today's workplace demotivators while invigorating the corporation with powerful, relevant employee motivators. Takes an organizational perspective to a traditionally individualistic topic—motivation. Offers a great technique to align individual desires with appropriate organizational motivators.

What America Does Right: Learning From Companies That Put People First by Robert Waterman, New York: W. W. Norton & Company, 1994. From the co-author of *In Search of Excellence,* a rather scholarly written, in-depth analysis of a few select companies. Powerful stories told in a personal account.

Index